The Validity Issue

WHAT SHOULD TEACHER CERTIFICATION TESTS MEASURE?

Edited by

Michael L. Chernoff
Paula M. Nassif
William Phillip Gorth

1987

LAWRENCE ERLBAUM ASSOCIATES, PUBLISHERS
Hillsdale, New Jersey   London

Lawrence Erlbaum Associates, Inc., Publishers
365 Broadway
Hillsdale, New Jersey 07642

ISBN 0-89859-947-4
LC card number   87-6804

Printed in the United States of America
10 9 8 7 6 5 4 3 2 1

CONTENTS

Preface

The chapters in this volume are based on presentations made at two major conferences. The first is one entitled *What Should Teacher Certification Tests Measure? The Validity Issue*, sponsored by National Evaluation Systems, Inc., in 1986 and held in San Francisco. This conference brought a number of professional educators together to discuss the validity question. The second source of chapters is a symposium on the teacher certification testing program in Texas conducted at the 1986 National Council on Measurement in Education convention. With one exception, the papers in this volume have not appeared in print before.

This book deals with an issue of critical interest to state education department program administrators and policy makers, deans and faculty members of colleges and departments of education, state legislators with a particular interest in education issues, and education professionals (teachers, district superintendents, etc.).

We believe this book contains a number of important discussions on a timely and compelling topic. We hope it proves valuable to the reader.

Acknowledgments

In creating this book on teacher certification testing issues, our principal debt is to the authors whose work appears herein. Not only did they provide the informative chapters, but they also calmly accepted our editorial changes.

At National Evaluation Systems, Carolyn Ayers and Nancy Seely undertook the major copyediting responsibilities for the book. The diverse sources of the chapters and the differing styles of the authors presented a challenge; their contribution toward a unified volume is deeply appreciated. We are also indebted to Sue Parent, Marketing Department Secretary who typed many of the original manuscripts; Cait Whittle, Manager of the Word Processing/ Typesetting Department; Julie Collins, Production Director; Heather Perry, Graphic Artist who designed the pages and the cover; Bonnie Forguites, Typesetter; and Brian Nelson, Production Editor.

We also appreciate the help and support of the staff at Lawrence Erlbaum Associates, particularly Carol Lachman and Jack Burton.

—Michael L. Chernoff for NES

Introduction

The Pressure Continues

In 1985, National Evaluation Systems, Inc. (NES) edited a book entitled *Testing for Teacher Certification* dealing with a range of issues associated with certification tests for prospective public school teachers. Since the publication of that work, there has been no diminution in pressure for these types of programs. If anything, such pressures have increased. Public opinion runs strongly in favor of tests for prospective teachers, and approximately 40 states have begun using some kind of test as a part of their certification procedures.

A SHIFT IN EMPHASIS

Until about a year ago, thinking on this topic was represented primarily by calls for reform. *A Nation at Risk: The Imperative for Educational Reform* (National Commission on Excellence in Education, 1983) is typical of the several reports that decried the state of public education in this country and spoke of the need for major reform. While tests for prospective teachers were but one aspect of that reform, their high visibility and controversial nature guaranteed them considerable attention.

The past year or so has been typified by plans and programs outlining the nature of those reforms. For example, the report of the Task Force on Teaching as a Profession, *A Nation Prepared: Teachers for the 21st Century* (1986), sponsored by the Carnegie Forum on Education and the Economy received a tremendous amount of general press coverage and notice in professional newsletters. The report contains an agenda and a list of suggestions for changes in educational policy and practice oriented exclusively toward the teaching profession.

Similarly, the report of the Holmes Group (1986), a group of deans of major institutions that train teachers, addresses issues concerning the preparation of teachers and their certification. The California Commission on the Teaching Profession (1985) issued a well-distributed document entitled *Who Will Teach Our Children? A Strategy for Improving California's Schools* (sometimes known as the Commons Report after the chair of the research committee), which is typical of efforts by individual states.

The concentration on teachers as a remedy to the challenges confronting American education is neither new nor unexpected.

What is different at this time, perhaps, is the emphasis on a demonstrated assurance that individuals entering a classroom possess the minimal qualifications for the performance of their duties. It is well worth noting in this regard that both the American Federation of Teachers and the National Education Association support the idea of examinations as a part of the credentialing process.

In short, there doesn't appear to be a slowdown in the debate over educational reform; an emphasis on accountability persists. The number of initiatives "on the table" has grown, including the creation of some type of national board that would develop and implement standards for the teaching profession across the country. Regardless of the outcome of that proposal, or any other particular proposal, it is indisputable that for the next several years we will witness an increase in the number of states testing prospective teachers and in the variety of programs oriented toward that task.

Purpose of this Book

The major focus of this volume is on the validity of teacher certification tests. The topic is one of interest to a number of audiences, albeit they approach the issue from slightly different perspectives.

- *State education department staff.* Clearly, those individuals responsible for setting policy and developing and implementing programs related to teacher certification have a necessary interest in the topic.

- *Teacher education institution faculty members and deans.* The institutions that prepare individuals for the teaching profession also have an obvious stake in programs that would test their students as a part of the certification process. This interest is accentuated by the fact that many of the recent reports (e.g., Carnegie Forum, Holmes Group) deal with testing as one aspect of teacher preparation. Indeed, the past year has seen increased attention to the nature and quality of teacher education.

- *The professional measurement community.* The validity of measurement is a traditional concern of this population. While any program can be discussed in terms of the number of different types of validity, the issue has provided grist for both theoretical and empirical mills for decades. Within this group are many whose particular interests are in licensing tests; this book will be of special interest to them.

- *Classroom teachers.* Within the past year, already certified classroom teachers in Texas and Arkansas have been tested. While this book focuses on the testing of prospective teachers (i.e., those who have not yet been certified), the topic of licensing requirements, and the potential expansion of testing to include currently certified teachers make the classroom teacher a logical reader of this book.

- *Legislators.* In many instances, the impetus for teacher certification testing programs comes from the state legislature. In some cases, the relevant legislation is general, stating only that tests of subject-matter knowledge shall be given. In other cases, the legislation provides more detail as to the nature of the instruments. Regardless of the circumstances, it would seem that policy writers at the legislative level can only benefit from an understanding of the issues involved. This book, which focuses on validity, may be of assistance to legislators contemplating new programs or evaluating current activities in their states.

Validity: The Critical Issue

To discuss the validity of a measurement instrument is to ask what it should measure, within the context of certification program goals. In teacher certification testing, the program seeks to assure that the welfare of the public is protected by establishing that practitioners in a given profession have met some predetermined standards of knowledge or performance. The logic behind such requirements is generally not disputed today.

That one might expect professionals to meet certain qualifications does not, however, specify what those qualifications are. Obviously, they are highly specific to the profession itself. In teaching, one might list a variety of personal attributes that would be deemed necessary for adequate classroom performance.

SUBJECT-MATTER KNOWLEDGE
Among such attributes would be knowledge of the subject matter one wishes to teach. It is the case that a deep and rich understanding of an academic discipline does not guarantee effective performance. On the other hand, it is certainly the case

that one is very unlikely to be an effective teacher without that subject-matter knowledge. Some argue that no paper-and-pencil test can predict teacher effectiveness in the classroom. We would agree, but in a qualified fashion. While subject-matter knowledge alone may not guarantee effective teaching, inadequate knowledge of the subject matter does, we believe, guarantee ineffectiveness.

It is difficult to argue how, regardless of other attributes, a person who does not know some minimum amount of content of a subject (e.g., biology) can hope to communicate that content effectively. Indeed, the individual would have nothing to communicate.

CRITERION-REFERENCED VALIDITY

It seems natural that measurement specialists and professional educators alike would wish to know the relationship between an individual's test score and the effectiveness of classroom performance. In fact, state agencies institute such testing programs in order to provide some assurance that individuals entering the classroom are capable of performing there.

Some observers would like to see more research on criterion-related validity (i.e., on the relationship between test scores and classroom performance). Unfortunately, the methodological difficulties surrounding such studies are numerous and complex. This introduction will not address those concerns in detail. A paper presented at the 1986 American Psychological Association Convention (*Criterion-Related Validity and Teacher Certification Testing*, by William P. Gorth) does discuss the problems inherent in such an effort. These problems are sufficiently severe to preclude such studies for a number of technical and political reasons. In addition, the American Educational Research Association/American Psychological Association/National Council on Measurement *Standards for Educational and Psychological Tests* (1985) indicates that criterion-referenced validity is generally not feasible for licensure programs.

CONTENT VALIDITY

The primary type of validity discussed in conjunction with teacher certification testing programs (and other professional credentialing examinations) is content validity. This refers to a relationship between what the test measures and the particular skills or knowledge required on the job. There should be, in short, a demonstrable relationship between the two. In the context of teacher certification tests of subject-matter knowledge, it is the responsibility of the test developer/sponsoring agency to demonstrate that the content knowledge measured by the test is content knowledge required for classroom performance.

The chapters in this volume that describe the teacher certification testing program in Texas note the process by which this relationship was empirically established.

The measurement of subject-matter knowledge does not, as noted above, constitute a complete inventory of those skills and knowledge necessary for teacher effectiveness. Subject-matter knowledge is a necessary, yet incomplete, assurance of classroom effectiveness. Tests of prospective teachers are one of a series of requirements including graduation from an approved preparation program and a successful teaching internship. It is the combination of such factors, each assessing the teacher candidate on specific dimensions, that makes for a more rounded portrait of an individual's credentials.

Hence, those who criticize paper-and-pencil tests of content knowledge for not addressing these other attributes are missing the point of such tests. The tests do not seek to measure interpersonal and other skills that are, undeniably, related to classroom performance. On the other hand, to dismiss subject-matter tests as irrelevant is to overlook a major facet of classroom performance—namely, knowledge of the subject matter in which one is providing instruction.

References

American Educational Research Association, American Psychological Association, & National Council on Measurement in Education. 1985. *Standards for educational and psychological tests.* Washington, DC: Author.

California Commission on the Teaching Profession. 1985. *Who will teach our children? A strategy for improving California's schools.* Sacramento: California Commission on the Teaching Profession.

Carnegie Forum on Education and the Economy. 1986. *A nation prepared: Teachers for the 21st century.* New York: Carnegie Corporation of New York.

Gorth, W. P., and Chernoff, M. L. (Eds.). 1986. *Testing for teacher certification.* Hillsdale, NJ: Lawrence Erlbaum Associates.

xiv

Gorth, W. P. (1986, April). *Criterion-related validity and teacher certification testing.* Paper presented at the convention of the American Psychological Association, San Francisco.

The Holmes Group. (1986). *Tomorrow's teachers: A report of the Holmes Group.* East Lansing, MI: Author.

National Commission on Excellence in Education. 1983. *A nation at risk: The imperative for educational reform.* Washington, DC: United States Government Printing Office.

Disparate Impact of Teacher Competency Testing on Minorities: Don't Blame the Test Takers—or the Tests *

Michael A. Rebell

Spurred by the recent spate of Commission reports that have decried the state of education in America,[1] many states have recently enacted legislation to raise educational standards. By 1984, over half of the states had implemented some form of standardized testing requirement to assess the competence of prospective teachers. By 1988, nine more will join their ranks.[2] In addition, a number of states have enacted legislation requiring incumbent teachers to prove their competence through standardized examinations.[3]

The trend toward standardized testing for teacher certification appears to be motivated by a widely held perception that many teacher candidates are ill prepared to undertake the critical function of educating the nation's youth. A good deal of evidence substantiates this perception. The lowered relative salary scales and diminished prestige of the teaching profession have reduced both the number and the qualifications of applicants to teacher training programs.[4] These factors have undermined the traditional system in which graduates of state-approved teacher training programs were presumed competent and were automatically granted state certification. In the wake of a perceived crisis, policy makers have begun to implement a number of educational reforms.

The long-range solution to the problem of teacher competence clearly requires increasing teacher salaries, enhancing the status of the profession, and raising the caliber of teacher training programs' academic offerings. Some of these reforms, most notably salary increases, have already begun to be instituted. While long-range measures are being considered, however, the strong political demand for immediate assurance of competence in the classroom is being placated by implementing standardized testing requirements. These tests are politically appealing because they

Michael A. Rebell is a Founding Partner of Rebell & Katzive of New York.

*A version of this chapter was originally published in the *Yale Law & Policy Review*. It is printed here with the permission of the author and original publisher.

provide a quick, relatively inexpensive mechanism for weeding out
unqualified teacher candidates and because they promise to impose
objective external standards.

QUESTIONS REGARDING TESTS

Standardized testing of teachers, however, raises a number of
significant questions: Can a battery of pen-and-paper tests truly
assess the full range of skills needed to perform effectively in the
classroom? If a test purports to cover only knowledge of minimum
subject-matter content, is it a fair criterion for certification, or
should college grade point averages or performance evaluations
also enter into the equation? If these are generally valid, are they
differentially biased against particular minority groups? Most of
the recent political and legal controversy has focused on the last
of these questions because of the highly adverse impact the tests
have had on minorities. That thousands of black and Hispanic
students who have prepared for teaching careers are being denied
entrance certification to a profession in which minorities are
already underrepresented is a serious and pressing social issue.
Needless to say, the disparate impact of teacher certification tests
on minority candidates has generated a substantial amount of
litigation.

DISPARATE IMPACT

In this chapter, I will describe the extent of the disparate impact
suffered by minority candidates and explore the general legal
standards for validating tests that have an adverse impact on
minority applicants. Under current case law, most certification tests
would pass muster despite their impact on minorities. I will trace
the development of two new legal theories which, however, if they
are widely accepted by the courts, might invalidate many of the
tests.

I will argue that these new legal theories exacerbate rather than
solve the problem. Low minority pass rates do not reflect either
bias in the tests or lack of aptitude in the candidates, but are a
result of substantial underlying deficiency in the candidates'
academic preparation. Especially in the Deep South where most
of the disparate impact has been felt, educational shortfalls stem
not only from teacher training programs, but also from the entire
legacy of inferior, segregated schooling. To certify a wave of well-
intentioned but ill-prepared teacher candidates would only
perpetuate the cycle of unequal educational opportunity.

Accordingly, the objective standards reflected in the tests must be maintained as critical accountability measures in order to compel long-range reform of educational offerings to university students. In the short run, motivated candidates who fail on a first attempt should be provided with intensive remedial opportunities to assist them in improving their skills so that they eventually obtain certification. These recommendations will be considered at greater length below.

Disparate Impact and Test Validation

The extent of the disparate impact of teacher certification examinations on minority candidates is evident from the results of the first administration of the California Basic Educational Skills Test (CBEST, developed by the Educational Testing Service) in 1983. While 76 percent of the white candidates passed, the pass rate for minority candidates was markedly lower. Only 26 percent of blacks, 38 percent of Mexican Americans, and 50 percent of Asian Americans passed the test.[5] Recent teacher certification tests in the Deep South produced similar outcomes. Results of the 1983 National Teacher Examination (NTE) in Louisiana and the 1983 Florida Teacher Certification Exam show respectively a 78 percent and 90 percent pass rate for whites, but only a 15 percent and 35 percent pass rate for blacks.[6] If these trends continue, "minority representation in the national teaching force could be reduced to less than 5 percent by 1990."[7]

NEW PROFESSIONAL OPPORTUNITIES

Part of the problem revealed by these disturbing statistics can be traced to heavy demands on the available talent pool. As noted above, minority students' interest in teaching has declined significantly in the past fifteen years as new career opportunities outside education have become available to them for the first time.[8] Nevertheless, the scope of the disparate pass rates, and their impact on the lives of thousands of individuals whose entry into their chosen career is blocked off, cannot be ignored. The results of recent litigation guarantee that the problem will not go unnoticed. Courts in Alabama, Arkansas, and Texas are currently considering these issues and other suits are sure to follow.

PAST CASES

Challenges to teacher certification tests are not new. In the 1970s, a wave of litigation in the Deep South challenged the use of the NTE as a certification device. The NTE is an examination which was created by the Educational Testing Service (ETS) to assess students' knowledge of the typical curricula taught at teacher training institutions throughout the country. ETS did not recommend or authorize the use of the NTE as a certification device in any particular state since the exam had not been validated for this purpose. Under these conditions, courts did not hesitate to enjoin use of the NTE as a certification or job retention requirement where it was shown to have the effect of denying continued employment to black teachers in newly desegregated school systems.[9] The current generation of testing litigation, however, raises more difficult legal and policy issues. Most of the recently implemented testing requirements have been adopted as part of a broad education reform program, rather than for clearly discriminatory reasons. Moreover, most tests have been professionally developed and extensive efforts have been undertaken to validate them for the specific purposes for which they are being used.[10]

Motivation for Testing

Of course, despite stated benign purposes, the fact that a state education department adopts a testing program which is likely to have a substantial disparate impact on minority candidates can raise questions concerning the motivation behind the reforms, especially if the state in question is one with a history of *de jure* segregation. Under such circumstances, it is possible that a state might have adopted all or part of a professionally developed testing program as a sophisticated device with which to perpetuate or even extend past discriminatory hiring practices.

On the other hand, if the remaining vestiges of racial segregation are to be overcome, it is necessary to break the cycle of failure that has caused low minority achievement rates on standardized tests. Allowing ill-prepared individuals to teach youngsters in the predominantly minority schools to which the less qualified teachers tend to be assigned will perpetuate historical patterns of unequal opportunities indefinitely.[11] In order to ensure that the next generation of minority students receives competent instruction, high standards for teacher competency must be maintained.[12] This is so despite the fact that insistence upon high standards has an unfortunate immediate impact on present minority candidates who, often through no fault of their own, were not properly trained or given fair opportunities to prepare for a demanding professional career.

Standardized tests are criticized because they cannot measure personal warmth and caring, the ability to maintain order, and other qualities important for effective teaching. Well-constructed tests, however, can measure a candidate's basic knowledge of the subject matter at hand, knowledge which is indisputably a *sine qua non* for competent teaching. It may eventually become possible to develop more effective tools for objectively measuring the broad range of skills, personal traits, instructional techniques, and subject-matter knowledge that is required. That such broad-based evaluative techniques are not currently available does not mean that the more limited objective measures of minimum subject-matter competency which we do have should not be used. As Nathan Glazer has said: "It is easy to attack tests: the question is whether there is an alternative. Tests correlate roughly with some kind of ability. . . . To attempt to introduce other qualities means to depend on the uncertain outcomes of interviews and other kinds of qualitative assessment."[13]

Teacher competency testing is not the only context in which standardized tests have raised these issues. Such tests are used for many purposes and have resulted in disparate impact on minorities in many other situations. The courts have therefore had to wrestle extensively in recent years with the issue of what level of test validation should be required when minorities are detrimentally affected. For the most part, the courts have scrutinized the tests under Title VII of the 1964 Civil Rights Act, the major federal statute prohibiting discrimination in employment.[14] The statute allows an employer to use "a professionally developed ability test" only if it is not "designed, intended or used" for discriminatory purposes.[15]

Validation

The requirements for test validation developed by the courts and the regulatory agencies in response to Title VII tend to be accepted as the general operative standards for all employment-related tests. It is not clear, however, whether all licensing and certification examinations that are prerequisites for employment are "employment tests" under Title VII.[16] Whether or not Title VII

technically applies to teacher certification tests, well-developed
minimum subject competency tests have little difficulty meeting
its validation standards.

TITLE VII STANDARDS

The Title VII validation standards are set forth in guidelines that
have been issued by the Federal Equal Employment Opportunity
Commission (EEOC).[17] These guidelines were cited approvingly and
applied by the Supreme Court in *Griggs v. Duke Power Company*[18]
and a series of later decisions.[19] Validation under the EEOC
Guidelines falls into several categories, the most significant of which
are "criterion-related validation" and "content validation."[20]
Criterion-related validation generally requires an employer using
a test to demonstrate that those examinees who pass the test or
receive higher grades on it perform better on the job than those
who fail or get lower grades. In other words, it usually requires
empirical evidence that the test actually predicts competency on
the job. In the teacher certification context, criterion-related
validation would require a showing that those exhibiting greater
knowledge and skills on the test actually perform better in the
classroom. It is generally acknowledged that the current state of
the art of test measurement ("psychometrics") cannot achieve
accurate predictive correlations of this type.

CONTENT VALIDATION

The alternative validation approach, "content validation," requires
the employer to show that the content of a test is reasonably related
to the knowledge and skills required for effective performance on
the job. In the teacher testing context, minimal subject-matter
competency tests which include some, if not all, of the knowledge
needed for effective teaching, would be assessed under a content
validation standard. Although earlier versions of the EEOC
Guidelines contained an explicit preference for criterion-related
validation, under the current *Guidelines* either validation procedure
is considered equally acceptable. Therefore, content-based tests,
if properly developed, would be acceptable under the *Guidelines*
even if they had a substantial adverse impact on minority
applicants.

In the early years of enforcement of Title VII and the EEOC
Guidelines, many employment tests which had a disparate impact
on minorities were invalidated by the courts. Those cases are,
however, largely irrelevant to the current crop of teacher
certification tests. Most of the invalidated tests were *ad hoc* selection

devices. No serious attempts had been made to analyze the requirements of the job and correlate test content with them.[21] As companies and public employers became more aware of the legal requirements and more sophisticated in their use of testing devices, the trend shifted dramatically; after 1976, the tests were validated in many more cases.[22]

DECISIONS SUPPORTING TESTS

The U.S. Supreme Court's 1976 decision in *Washington v. Davis*[23] further influenced the trend toward upholding the use of employment tests, even those with a disparate impact. There, the Court upheld the use of a verbal ability test for police recruits despite its disparate impact on minority applicants and its failure to meet a technical requirement of the EEOC *Guidelines*. Although the Court found that the EEOC *Guidelines* were not directly applicable in *Davis*, it seemed willing to accept a lower standard than that of the EEOC's because the case involved a professionally developed testing program that had been adopted in good faith by a public employer.[24] This attitude was further evidenced by the Supreme Court's later summary affirmance, in *United States v. South Carolina*, of a three-judge district court's approval of the South Carolina NTE examination despite a strong disparate impact on minority candidates.[25]

In sum, the EEOC *Guidelines*' inclusion of content validation techniques as an alternative methodology, together with the lower standard applied by the Supreme Court where public employers have made good faith attempts to use professionally developed tests, suggests that properly developed teacher certification tests are likely to be upheld by the courts even if they have substantial disparate impact on minority applicants. Moreover, since these are "licensing" tests and are imbued with a significant public policy purpose (protecting the public from incompetent practitioners), the courts are likely to be even more deferential to defendants than they are in the strict employment context.[26]

NEW LEGAL THEORIES

Plaintiffs in the current teacher competency testing cases, unhappy with the existing standards, have developed two significant new legal theories that would hold state certification boards to higher validation requirements than the Supreme Court has endorsed. The first, "instructional validation," demands that test content be geared to the curricula of teacher training colleges. The second would require the deletion from examinations of questions on which minorities do not score well. If these concepts are accepted by the courts, either teacher competency tests will have to be abandoned or fundamental alterations will have to be made in test standards to accommodate the present level of minority candidates' preparation. Neither of these approaches is desirable as a matter of policy or justified as a matter of law.

Instructional Validation

STUDENT COMPETENCY TESTING

The Supreme Court has not explored test validation concepts since its major rulings a decade ago. Thus, the lower federal courts have been called upon to apply—and possibly extend—the Title VII test validation standards without specific guidance from the Court. One area in which the lower federal courts have extended Title VII concepts, even though technically the statute does not apply, is student competency testing. In *Debra P. v. Turlington*,[27] a student testing case, the court of appeals developed the concept of "instructional validation."[28] Because this concept may become a major issue in the teacher certification area, *Debra P.* must be examined in some detail.

DEBRA P.

The *Debra P.* litigation was part of a concerted effort by the Harvard Center on Law and Education and other advocacy groups to challenge minimum competency statutes which have been adopted in recent years by more than two-thirds[29] of the states. Minimum competency testing involves the use of standardized testing instruments to assess student mastery of "basic skills," usually reading, writing, and mathematics. While standardized achievement tests have been used in secondary education for years, the minimum competency testing programs are new in that they are being implemented on a statewide basis to prescribe remedial help or deny high school diplomas to students who fail the tests. Minimum competency tests (MCTs) tend to have a substantial disparate impact on minority students.[30]

At issue in *Debra P.* was the Florida "functional literacy examination," which had had a substantial adverse impact on minority students. The first time this test was administered, 78 percent of the black students but only 25 percent of the white students failed one or both sections.[31] In light of these statistics, the district court closely examined whether the test met the validation requirements.[32]

Because of Florida's long history of *de jure* school segregation, the court paid special attention to the plaintiff's allegations of intentional discrimination. It rejected the contention that the state commissioner's knowledge of the effects of the test on black school children necessarily constituted intentional discrimination. On the contrary, the court applauded Florida's motives in implementing a testing program to raise educational standards:

> The legitimate interest in implementing a test to evaluate the established state-wide objectives is obvious. The minimal objectives established could be continually upgraded and the test could be utilized not only to gauge achievement, but also to identify deficiencies for the purpose of remediation.[33]

At the same time, however, the court also concluded that:

> The timing of the program must be questioned to some extent because it sacrifices through the diploma sanction a large percentage of black twelfth-grade students in the rush to implement the legislative mandate.[34]

Accordingly, the court enjoined Florida from requiring passage of the examination as a requirement for graduation for a period of four years.[35]

INSTRUCTIONAL VALIDITY

On appeal, the court accepted the lower court's basic findings and affirmed its holding that the test items were not biased, but went beyond the EEOC test validation concepts upon which the district court had relied. It held that an additional requirement should be imposed upon student competency tests, namely a showing of "instructional validity."[36] Specifically, the state was required to prove that the "test covered things actually taught in the classrooms."[37] Because the lower court had not considered whether the "instructional validity" of the test had been established, the case was remanded.

IMPLEMENTATION PROBLEMS

The court of appeals' application of the doctrine of instructional validity in this decision has generated substantial interest in psychometric circles.[38] There is a widespread assumption that instructional validity has become a judicial requirement for student competency tests and perhaps for tests in related fields such as teacher certification as well.[39] This assumption, however, overlooks the difficulty encountered by the district court when it attempted to implement the instructional validation standard. Practical and conceptual problems, clearly revealed in the record of the remand proceedings, led the district and appeals courts to become markedly more circumspect. The implications of the courts' post-remand consideration of the issue have not been sufficiently appreciated.

Although there is an obvious common-sense appeal to the notion that students should not be penalized for failing to test well on subject matter they have not been taught, the *Debra P.* remand hearing shows that any attempt to determine what individual students have actually been taught is impossible. In order to establish that every student in the state had had a fair opportunity to learn each of the many subjects covered by an examination, the practices of every school district, perhaps even of every school and classroom, in the state over the twelve-year span of a public school education would have to be analyzed.[40] Arguably, the need to demonstrate that a fair opportunity had been provided to each student could be sidestepped by aggregating experiences in order to show that the concepts covered on the tests were taught consistently throughout the state. This would pose serious problems in terms of individual rights, however. Moreover, limited review, even if doctrinally acceptable, would be an unmanageable enterprise that would intrude upon ongoing educational operations. The programs of hundreds of school districts would have to be assessed over extended periods of time.[41] Educators are also not likely to welcome such an undertaking because "attempts to assess [instructional] validity on a statewide basis [could] lead to debilitating bureaucracy, costly administration, and stifling of educational innovation."[42]

VALIDATION STUDY

The *Debra P.* remand decision brought these practical problems into sharp focus. In response to the court of appeals' decision, Florida retained a consulting firm to undertake an extensive four-part validation study. A teacher survey was sent to 65,000 teachers. A detailed survey of all of Florida's school districts and four university laboratories was taken. Site visit teams were sent to each of the school districts to follow up on the surveys. Thousands of student surveys were completed. Despite this comprehensive range of data, the plaintiffs argued that the validation study was fundamentally flawed because the survey was constructed to invite positive responses from teachers. They also asserted that the survey was deficient because it covered only one rather than all twelve years of the students' education, and because it provided insufficient evidence of what actually happens in the classroom.

The district court's response revealed its frustration with instructional validation:

> [A]bsent viewing a videotape of every student's school career, how can we know what really happened to each child? Even assuming that such videotapes were available, how could this Court decide, in constitutional terms, which students received appropriate instruction and which did not? Suppose that there is one student who never encountered a teacher who taught the SSAT-II skills, or a teacher who taught the skills well, should the entire test be declared invalid? What if the number of students were 3,000 rather than 1?[43]

CURRICULAR VALIDITY

In light of these difficulties, the district court abandoned the strict requirements of instructional validation and instead upheld the examination on a significantly more limited basis, a requirement of "curricular validity."[44] The court explained, "What is required is that the skills be included in the official curriculum and that the majority of the teachers recognize them as being something they should teach."[45] In other words, as long as the curriculum included the basic objectives and the teachers were aware of them, the court would not insist on the more stringent instructional validity requirement that students had actually received instruction in each of the requisite objectives.

When the appeals court affirmed this holding, it also seemed less committed to instructional validity: "The experts conceded that there are no accepted educational standards for determining whether a test is instructionally valid."[46] While the decision affirmed the district court's findings of fact as not "clearly erroneous," it was carefully qualified. It specifically eschewed the difficult task of establishing a clear legal standard. In sum, the court of appeals appeared to have studied the complex record of the remand proceedings below, realized the difficulties involved, and limited rather than extended the lower court holding.[47]

Teacher Competency Testing

Despite the difficulties experienced by the courts in attempting to implement "instructional validation" in the student testing context, the concept has been widely invoked by plaintiffs challenging teacher certification tests. Instructional validation here would require that certification examinations correlate with the curriculum at the teacher training institutions, not to the knowledge and skills needed for competent teacher performance in the classroom.[48] The notion that candidates for teacher certification should be tested only on material to which they were exposed at their training institutions is appealing. Nevertheless, abstract equity must be weighed against the virtual impossibility of proving what was taught at each of the many teacher training institutions in every state. (Instructional validation could even require states to consider the curricula of out-of-state institutions candidates had attended.) Moreover, the rights of the public school students who will ultimately be taught by the candidates must be considered. The equity issue is problematic because the interests of teaching candidates must be weighed against the equal, arguably greater, interests of future minority students who are entitled to be taught by competent teachers.

The analogy between the student testing in *Debra P.* and the current teacher testing situation is even more tenuous when considered in light of applicable legal doctrines. *Debra P.* was based in large part on the due process notion of the "legitimate expectation" of high school students that they would receive a diploma if they passed all their courses and otherwise met the standards which were in effect prior to the implementation of the competency testing requirement. Candidates for teacher certification do not have such a "legitimate expectation" because simply attending school for four years does not entitle them to a teaching license. The concept of state credentialing is based squarely on the propositions that the public must be protected against incompetent practitioners and that no one has a right to enter the profession without demonstrating the requisite degree of competence.[49]

In short, because of tenuous doctrinal support and serious practical proof problems, there is little basis for extending instructional validation to teacher certification. Moreover, it is doubtful that the courts will do so.[50] Even without any direct mandate, however, instructional validity has begun to influence the development of teacher certification testing. State education departments are including an instructional validation component in their test construction procedures in order to avoid possible legal challenges. This undermines the purpose of teacher competency testing and content validation standards which base certification on demonstrated classroom competence rather than on familiarity with the often substandard teacher training curricula. The plight of teacher certification candidates who have attended training institutions that do not adequately prepare them for their chosen professions is real and should be addressed. Their needs would be better met, however, by providing them with greater opportunity to prepare for the examination.

Following the Golden Rule: The Item Bias Approach

There is another emerging approach to competency testing which threatens to undermine the maintenance of competency standards by teacher certification tests. Known as the "Golden Rule" approach, this new concept could have serious adverse effects on the integrity of testing.

Under Title VII and the EEOC *Guidelines*, employment selection tests which have an adverse impact on minorities may be adopted if the employer can show that reasonable psychometric methods were used in the tests' construction. In other words, in the absence of a showing of intentional discrimination, adherence to the validation requirements set forth in the *Guidelines* establishes a presumption that the adverse impact did not result from discriminatory practices.[51]

Even where sound validation practice has been followed, however, an employer has an obligation to consider the use of suitable alternative selection procedures if another method with less adverse impact on minorities exists and is "substantially equally valid for a given purpose."[52] This provision is rarely applied because few alternative testing methods, especially for subject-matter competence, have been developed by the testing industry. Virtually all standardized certification tests, whatever the form of their validation, have tended to have substantial adverse impact on minority candidates.[53]

Item Bias Approach

Recently, however, certain new techniques for potentially reducing adverse impact on minorities have been proposed to the courts. These techniques eliminate specific examination questions ("items") on which minorities fare poorly. This approach does not take into account either the overall structure of the test or the basic constructs being tested. It focuses instead on the fact that certain test items in an otherwise acceptable test may prove more difficult for one group than for another. Elimination of "biased" items and the substitution of alternative items covering the same basic content is supposed to provide equity to all test takers while assuring an objective measure of relative or absolute competence.

GOLDEN RULE SETTLEMENT

The item bias approach received significant support when it was incorporated into a consent decree in *Golden Rule Insurance Company v. Washburn,* a decree into which ETS entered.[54] This protracted case was brought against ETS and the Illinois Department of Insurance by five people who had failed the Illinois Insurance Licensing Exam and by Golden Rule Insurance Company which claimed to have had trouble finding licensed minority agents to sell insurance in minority communities. Plaintiffs introduced preliminary evidence indicating that 78 percent of the white test takers passed the life insurance test, in contrast to only 65 percent of black test takers, and that 82 percent of the white test takers passed the accident and health insurance test, compared to 55 percent of the black test takers.[55]

ITEM CATEGORIES

The core of the *Golden Rule* settlement was a requirement that all items used on various administrations of the test be analyzed and classified into the following two categories:

1. Type I—those items for which (a) the correct-answer rates of black examinees, white examinees, and all examinees are not lower than forty percent (40%) at the .05 level of statistical significance, and (b) the correct-answer rates of black examinees and white examinees differ by no more than fifteen (15) percentage points at the .05 level of statistical significance; or

2. Type II—all other items.[56]

After this classification had been accomplished, the decree then required ETS to assemble new test forms "in accordance with the subject matter coverage and weighting of the applicable content outline," pursuant to the following guidelines:

1. Type I Items shall be used exclusively so long as they are available in sufficient numbers.

2. Those Type I Items for which the correct-answer rates of black examinees and white examinees differ least shall be used first.

3. Type II Items may be used, and shall be used before any new items. . . may be used, to the extent Type I Items are not available in sufficient numbers.

4. To the extent it is necessary to use Type II Items, those Type II Items for which the correct-answer rates of black examinees and white examinees differ the least shall be used first.[57]

In short, *Golden Rule* requires ETS to use questions on which blacks as a group tend to perform as well as whites before it uses items on which the performance differential is greater.

On its face, the settlement appears relatively innocuous. It permits Illinois to continue to use insurance licensing examinations. It indirectly endorses ETS' validation methods and permits the company to assemble tests from its existing item banks. All that is specifically required is that items be drawn from the overall pool in a certain designated order.

POTENTIAL DISTORTION

Upon further analysis, however, the *Golden Rule* approach raises a number of serious concerns. The major problem involves the distortion of the proportionate weight of subject matter covered by an exam which is established by the content validation process to reflect "on-the-job" competence requirements. The weighting of the different subjects covered by the exam is known as "the blueprint." If many items necessary for the test blueprint are eliminated or modified, the integrity of this blueprint may be jeopardized. For example, if an analysis of a high school mathematics teacher's job indicates that 20 percent of her time will be spent teaching geometry, the test blueprint will require that 20 percent of the items on the test cover geometry. If blacks as a group fare relatively poorly on questions dealing with geometry, elimination of those items from the test will raise their scores. However, elimination of these items will also distort the validity of the test as an indicator of the competence of all teachers certified in mathematics to perform adequately on the job.[58]

"ESSAY" TOPICS

Test content may be further distorted by the preference of the *Golden Rule* approach for easy items. "Type I" items are more likely to be "easy" since questions that *all* groups answer correctly will not exhibit high differential statistics. Accordingly, difficult concepts will be measured less often, even if such concepts are an important measure of ability to perform on the job. Finally, the item bias approach may invite negative psychological and political reactions from white candidates who feel the technique is unfair because it eliminates questions on which they do well. This reaction is not unreasonable since current evidence indicates that the specific items eliminated under item bias techniques do not have any apparent culturally or racially based wording or content.[59]

In response to some of these concerns, ETS has attempted to minimize the significance of the *Golden Rule* settlement. An ETS spokesman concluded, "[T]here is nothing in the settlement requiring us to drop questions. . . The way we do business now has basically been confirmed."[60] Plaintiffs, however, interpreted the settlement differently. They heralded it as a major breakthrough: "[It is] a significant victory in the effort to eliminate discrimination in our country. . . [I]t is likely. . . that students taking the SAT and GRE will want similar safeguards, now that they know it can be done."[61] Plaintiffs also noted the legal significance of the *Golden Rule* formula as "an alternative method" which would have to be considered by all developers of licensing or certification tests under the EEOC *Guidelines*. An expert psychologist retained by plaintiffs remarked that he expected the settlement to force ETS to revise its other tests because "once you have this method, to not use it is to knowingly use a more discriminatory test."[62]

The Golden Rule Approach in Teacher Certification Testing

Widespread publicity about the settlement within the testing industry and a general awareness of the legal requirement to use alternative selection methods have created an item bias bandwagon. Test makers are considering the *Golden Rule* approach when they develop new licensing examinations. Legislation to mandate the technique is pending in several states. Lawyers have begun to apply the concept in pending cases; for example, it was central to the recent Alabama teacher certification case consent decree.[63]

ALABAMA

The Alabama settlement, the validity of which is still being litigated,[64] not only adopted the *Golden Rule* method but substantially extended it. The settlement requires division of all items in the teacher competency test into three categories: Type I contains items with black/white performance differentials of no more than 5 percent; Type II contains items with ranges between 5-10 percent; and Type III consists of items ranging between 10-15 percent. In general, however, only the Type I and II items could be used in actual tests; inclusion of Type III items would be permitted only after the pool of Type I and II items had been exhausted, and, even then, no more than 10 percent of the total number of questions could be Type III. Items with a differential ratio above 15 percent could never be used.[65]

In sum, the 15 percent differential analysis concept used in *Golden Rule* to classify items for order of use was extended in the Alabama settlement to preclude use of any items falling outside that 15 percent range. Essentially, the Alabama approach precludes use of any items having substantial adverse impact on minority candidates. Thus, the limited item bias approach of the Illinois case established a precedent that blossomed into a substantially more radical form in its very next application.

Given the political pressures to reduce the adverse impact of teacher certification exams, and the extensive advocacy campaign being mounted to adopt and extend the *Golden Rule* formula, it seems likely that the radical Alabama version rather than the limited Illinois approach will become the predominant mode. Should the courts explicitly endorse the technique, especially the Alabama version, the item bias procedure might well be used as a valid alternative under EEOC *Guidelines*, requiring its consideration and possibly its adoption in all teacher certification situations.

EROSION OF PUBLIC INTEREST

Such use of the item bias approach could compromise the basic purpose of teacher certification testing. The blueprinting distortions and the tendency to use easier items which is inherent in the technique would ensure certification of more applicants—both minority and nonminority—without assessing their competence by meaningful objective standards.[66] Job access would be provided to more minority candidates, but at the cost of undermining certification standards and possibly lowering the quality of education of future generations of school children. Clearly, the public interest and ultimately the interest of the ill-prepared minority candidates themselves would be better served by pursuing reforms that would maintain the integrity of the tests.

Recommendations and Conclusion

Although legal challenges to teacher competency tests on behalf of minority applicants appear to be proliferating, influential black leaders in the education community are speaking out against the antitesting stance. Bernard R. Gifford, Dean of the Graduate School

of Education at the University of California at Berkeley, for
example, has argued that devaluing standardized tests evades the
serious issues raised by high minority failure rates and will only
perpetuate the problem.[67] Similarly, Mary H. Futrell, President of
the National Education Association, an organization that had
previously taken a public stand in opposition to teacher certification
testing, recently stated:

> I've heard some say that pre-service testing may hurt women and
> minorities. . . As a black woman, I don't buy that. As a matter of
> fact, I resent it. If we set clear and demanding expectations and then
> help all potential teachers reach those expectations, we can have
> both quality and equality.[68]

In short, these black leaders agree that, in the long run,
maintenance of educational standards and of the integrity of
certification tests will benefit both minority students and minority
teachers.[69]

Extending instructional validation or the *Golden Rule* technique
to teacher competency tests may, in the short run, raise minority
passing rates, but it will ultimately undermine the reformers'
efforts. Advocates for minority rights would be better advised to
press a reform agenda to meet Gifford and Futrell's call for raising
the substantive achievement level of minority applicants.[70] Such
reforms should have two major components. As a short-term
program, states should provide minority students with specific test
preparation assistance. In the long term, the basic educational
opportunities afforded minorities must be improved.[71]

BETTER PREPARATION AND REMEDIATION

In all competency testing situations, extensive preparatory
materials such as study guides, sample questions, and counseling
should be provided at state expense for minority students who have
not had an opportunity to develop sophisticated test-taking skills.
More important, an extensive program of remedial assistance aimed
at improving skills in areas of identifiable weaknesses should be
offered to all who fail an initial administration of the test.[72] Where
necessary, such a program might also provide funding for
additional semesters of study to help committed candidates reach
objective competency levels. Candidates should also be granted
multiple opportunities to retake the test.

HIGHER EDUCATION PROGRAMS

This meaningful reform approach could also eliminate many of
the problems posed by "instructional validation." I have argued in

this chapter that when there is a disparity between classroom job requirements and curriculum content at a teacher training institution, the job analysis requirements should prevail. There is no reason, however, why this disparity should exist. Institutions which purport to be dedicated to teacher training should gear their curriculum content to include, at a minimum, basic on-the-job competency requirements. State universities and teacher training colleges should be required to analyze their curricula and to gear curricular content to the job-related objectives of teacher certification examinations. Private institutions with curriculum offerings not substantially correlated with the job-related objectives established for state teacher certification examinations should be required to disclose this lack of correlation. Applicants for admission would then at least have notice that a degree from the institution would not be likely to provide them with thorough preparation for the state licensing examination.[73]

ADVANCED NOTIFICATION

Teacher candidates should also be given sufficient notice that a job-related teacher certification exam will be required. In *Debra P.*, the court enjoined implementation of Florida's student competency testing program for a four-year period in order to provide fair notice and an opportunity to prepare for the examinations to minority students who earlier in their school career had been victims of state-imposed segregation of the school system. Fairness requires adequate notice.[74] A similar due process concept was raised by the District Court in *United States v. Texas* but was reversed by the Court of Appeals for the Fifth Circuit.[75]

Reasonable notice requirements should apply to all teacher competency tests. Basic equity considerations, if not constitutional due process requirements, call for special efforts to be made to maximize notice and opportunities for preparation when new standardized testing programs are initiated. The amount of notice considered reasonable will, of course, depend on the circumstances of the particular testing program. If the new program constitutes a radical departure from the past (for example, if newly promulgated competency standards were not previously an established part of the state teacher training college curriculum) a lead-in period equal to the length of the teacher training program would appear appropriate. In other situations (for example, when a testing program standardizes long-standing requirements), a one- or two-year notice period might be adequate.

The Long-Term Solution

Reasonable notice and enhanced test preparation should enable more minority candidates, especially those close to the cut-score mark, to pass the tests. In the long term, however, the problem of the disparate impact of competency tests on minority candidates will only be solved by substantially upgrading the quality of education they receive. The failure rate for graduates of the predominantly black teacher training institutions in the South on teacher competency tests is disproportionately high relative not only to white candidates, but also to minority candidates attending integrated or predominantly white institutions.[76] The reason for this disparity is simple: all of these institutions emerged from dual higher education systems. The legacy of inferior facilities and faculties which the predominantly black institutions inherited endures despite somewhat increased funding levels in recent years.[77]

SUPPORTING BLACK INSTITUTIONS

Some might argue that, given this bleak record, it would be better to close down the predominantly black institutions and steer minority applicants to predominantly white campuses.[78] Despite the seeming logic of this approach, it should not be pursued. The predominantly black schools are the only avenue of opportunity available to thousands of minority students who, due to the inferior education provided to them in their early years, might not meet the entrance standards at more competitive institutions. Predominantly black colleges in the South must therefore be supported as they meet the needs of thousands of highly motivated minority students. The anticipated severe teacher shortage projected for the next decade, especially of minority teachers, provides an additional rationale for such support. In order to provide real opportunity to the students at these colleges, the caliber of their faculty and the quality of their offerings must be enhanced and their funding levels substantially increased.[79]

AFFIRMATIVE ACTION ADMISSIONS

Improving predominantly black institutions in the South is only part of the long-term solution. In both the South and the North, affirmative action to assist minority students attending predominantly white teacher training institutions is also essential. Special scholarship programs that provide support and incentives to minority students who meet standards at competitive institutions must be expanded. To this end, Dean Gifford has proposed a plan which is currently under consideration by the California State Legislature. Gifford's plan would identify minority and low-income students who are committed to teaching and provide them with intensive university and postgraduate training. The plan also includes programs and rewards for outstanding teachers, nonminority as well as minority.[80]

ROLE OF THE COURTS

A final observation which must be made when considering any solution to the disparate impact of teacher certification tests on minority teacher candidates concerns the role of the courts in the development of professional standards. As they become immersed in institutional reform, courts are increasingly involved in determining complex social science controversies. Although empirical studies indicated that judges are able to obtain and comprehend complex social and factual data,[81] the test validation and disparate impact issues raise new problems. Plaintiffs challenging teacher certification tests are asking judges not only to comprehend and apply established social science concepts, but to help formulate new professional standards.

Before *Debra P.* and *Golden Rule*, "instructional validity" and the "item bias analysis" were innovative suggestions which had been only tentatively raised in psychometric literature. They were not widely known, let alone widely accepted, before being thrust into prominence by the judicial process. Positive judicial imprimatur, even in a limited factual setting or in the confines of a settlement document, has conveyed an aura of legitimacy that substantially enhanced the professional acceptability of these concepts. Because of *Debra P.* and *Golden Rule*, these principles may become established fundamentals of professional judgment which must be carefully considered, if not adopted, by all practitioners in the psychometric field. The appearance of broad professional acceptance may well lead to further judicial invocation of these standards in future cases, on the assumption that they fairly reflect prevailing professional judgment in the field.[82]

Judges and professionals must recognize the interactive nature of this subtle process. Pronouncements of limited or qualified significance, based on professional understandings within one field, are overextended when too quickly translated into another. Given the dynamics of contemporary public policy formulation, judges can be important participants in the development of social science standards, and social scientists may have a legitimate interest in the development of a legal doctrine. The interrelationship between social science and legal standards in the area of standardized competency tests should not be furthered, however, until all participants are fully aware of the nature of the dialogue and of the impact each discipline has on the other.

Footnotes

1. *See, e.g.,* NATIONAL COMMISSION ON EXCELLENCE IN EDUCATION, A NATION AT RISK: THE IMPERATIVE FOR EDUCATIONAL REFORM (1983); E. BOYER, HIGH SCHOOL: A REPORT ON SECONDARY EDUCATION IN AMERICA (1983); J. GOODLAD, A PLACE CALLED SCHOOL: PROSPECTS FOR THE FUTURE (1984); MAKING THE GRADE: REPORT OF THE TWENTIETH CENTURY FUND TASK FORCE ON FEDERAL ELEMENTARY AND SECONDARY EDUCATION POLICY (1983); T. SIZER, HORACE'S COMPROMISE: THE DILEMMA OF THE AMERICAN HIGH SCHOOL (1984).

2. M. GOERTZ, R. EKSTROM & R. COLEY, THE IMPACT OF STATE POLICY ON ENTRANCE INTO THE TEACHING PROFESSION at 9 (Final Report, National Institute of Education Grant No. GA3-0073, 1984). The tests vary from state to state according to when they must be taken, i.e., prior, during, or after entry into a teacher training program. Also, some assess only basic skills or knowledge; others assess more extensive subject-matter mastery or classroom skills.

3. *See, e.g.,* 1983 ARK. ACTS 736; GA. CODE ANN. § 20-2-200(b)(1985); TEX. EDUC. CODE ANN § 13.047 (Vernon's 1986).

4. The number of college women majoring in education declined from 19 percent in 1972 to 10 percent in 1984; the number of men majoring in education declined from 6 percent to 3 percent during the same period. P. GARCIA, A STUDY ON TEACHER COMPETENCY TESTING AND TEST VALIDITY WITH IMPLICATIONS FOR MINORITIES at 7 (National Institute of Education Grant No. G-85-0004, 1985). Teachers-in-training ranked fourteenth out of sixteen occupational groups on SAT verbal scores and fifteenth out of sixteen on quantitative scores. Kirst, *Renewing the Teaching Profession,* STANFORD MAC., Spring 1985, at 52. Several prestigious institutions, including Yale, Harvard, Reed, and Duke, dropped their undergraduate teacher training programs in the 1970s. *Id.* at 53.

5. GARCIA, *supra* note 4, at Appendix C.

6. *Id.*

7. Smith, *The Critical Issue of Excellence and Equity in Competency Testing,* 35 J. OF TEACHER EDUC. 8 (1984).

8. Gifford, *Teacher Competency Testing and Its Effects on Minorities: Reflection and Recommendations* at 52 (Prepared for the 1984 ETS Conference on Educational Standards, Testing, and Access, 1985); Kirst, *supra* note 4 at 50.

9. *See, e.g.,* Baker v. Columbus Municipal Separate School District, 329 F. Supp. 706 (N.D. Miss. 1971), *aff'd* 462 F.2d 1112 (5th Cir. 1972); Walston v. County School Board of Nansemond County, 492 F.2d 919 (4th Cir. 1973); United States v. State of North Carolina, 400 F. Supp. 343 (E.D.N.C. 1975), *vacated* 425 F. Supp. 789 (E.D.N.C. 1977); Georgia Association of Educators v. Nix, 407 F. Supp. 1102 (N.D. Ga. 1976). *See also* Armstead v. Starkville Municipal Separate School District, 461 F.2d 276 (5th Cir. 1972) (requirement for minimum score on graduate record exam for initial appointment or retention of faculty positions invalidated).

10. Two types of teacher competency testing examinations are currently used. First is the NTE, which although it remains a standardized national examination of knowledge and skills taught in teacher training institutions is now generally validated by particular state or local school districts to insure that it reflects knowledge and skills needed in that particular setting. The second consists of "customized" examinations prepared by National Evaluation Systems, Inc. (NES) of Amherst, Massachusetts. The NES tests are based on job analyses conducted in each state to reflect local teaching requirements directly. *See* Flippo, *Teacher Certification Testing Across the United States and A Consideration of Some of the Issues* at 6, Tables 1 and 2 (Paper presented at annual meeting of American Educational Research Association, Chicago, 1985).

11. "I assume that the reason minority applicants fare worse on the test than Whites is that they themselves are victims of inferior schooling." Washington Post columnist William Raspberry quoted in Gifford, *supra* note 8 at 57. Gifford notes that major differentials in test scores also appear to be related to class bias factors as well as to race bias factors. He indicates that the College Board's *Profiles, College-Bound Seniors, 1983*, shows that "[T]he relationship between family income and test scores is highly significant. While not as high, the relationship between level of parental education and SAT scores of high school seniors is also very substantial." *Id.* at 56.

12. *See* generally GLAZER, *The Problem with Competence* in CHALLENGE TO AMERICAN SCHOOLS: THE CASE FOR STANDARDS AND VALUES (J. Bunzel, ed. 1985).

13. *Id.* at 227. Standardized minimum competency tests also provide a more objective assessment method than the unvalidated, often politically sensitive, traditional "program approval" certification approach. *See* Mehrens, *Validity Issues in Teacher Competency Tests*, Report Prepared for the Institute for Student Assessment and Evaluation, University of Florida (1986) at 8. Because teacher competency tests can provide some reliable information about the basic competence of applicants but cannot

provide a full rating of all pedagogical skills, test results should be used as a threshold eligibility requirement, and not as a method to rank applicants.

14.   42 U.S.C. § § 2000e to 2000e-15 (1982).

15.   42 U.S.C. § 2000e-2(h) (1982).

16.   *Compare, e.g.,* Tyler v. Vickery 517 F.2d 1089 (5th Cir. 1975); Woodard v. Virginia Board of Bar Examiners, 598 F.2d 1345, 1346 (4th Cir. 1979) (State Board of Bar Examiners is not an "employer" within the meaning of Title VII); *and* NOW v. Waterfront Commission of New York Harbor, 468 F. Supp. 317 (S.D.N.Y. 1979) (State waterfront licensing agency is not an employer); *with* Vanguard Justice Society v. Hughes, 471 F. Supp. 670, 696 (D. Md. 1979) (City civil service commission is the "employer" of police); *and* Puntolillo v. New Hampshire Racing Commission, 375 F. Supp. 1089 (D.N.H. 1974) (State racing commission is the "employer" of driver-trainers); *and* United States v. State of North Carolina, No. 4476 (E.D.N.C. June 23, 1982) (State Board of Education is the "employer" of local school district teachers).

17.   The *Guidelines*, which have been endorsed by the Justice Department, the Department of Labor and other federal agencies, are officially known as the Uniform Guidelines on Employee Selection Procedures (1978). They are codified at 29 C.F.R. Part 1607. The *Guidelines* specifically refer to the test validation standards contained in the *Standards for Educational and Psychological Testing,* Am. Psychological Ass'n, *et al.* (rev. ed. 1985).

18.   401 U.S. 424 (1971). The main holding in *Griggs* was that Title VII proscribes not only intentional discrimination, but also the use of tests which are neutral in intent but have a disparate impact on minorities. The Court held that tests resulting in a disparate impact may be used only if they are shown to be properly validated.

19.   *See especially,* Albemarle Paper Co. v. Moody, 422 U.S. 405 (1975). For a general overview of the case law concerning test validation, *see* M. REBELL & A. BLOCK, COMPETENCY ASSESSMENT AND THE COURTS: AN OVERVIEW OF THE STATE OF THE LAW, Prepared for the National Institute of Education, Contract NIE 400-78-0028 February 1980, and Note, *Minimum Competency Testing of Teachers for Certification: Due Process, Equal Protection and Title VII Implications,* 70 CORNELL L. REV. 494 (1985).

20.   The *Guidelines* also refer to a third category, "construct validation," which requires a showing that an examination measures identifiable traits, characteristics, or "constructs," that have been shown to be important to successful performance on the job. Construct validity is, however, less significant in actual practice and its application is often difficult to distinguish from content validation. *See, e.g.,* Guardians Ass'n of New York City v. Civil Service Comm'n, 630 F.2d 79 (2d Cir. 1980).

21.   *See,* REBELL & BLOCK, *supra* note 19, at 13. (Plaintiffs prevailed in 56 of 70 Title VII cases decided prior to 1976).

22. *Id.* at 22. (Plaintiffs prevailed in 18 of 37 cases decided after 1976).

23. 426 U.S. 229 (1976).

24. In *Washington v. Davis*, Title VII technically did not apply because the case was filed prior to 1972, when Title VII was extended to cover state and municipal employees. Strictly applied, although a positive correlation had been shown between success on the test and performance in the police academy training program, 426 U.S. at 246, the *Guidelines* would have required a further showing of a correlation between the requirements of the training program and success on the job. *See* 29 C.F.R. § 1607.4(c) (1975). The Court's relaxed attitude was partly due to the fact that the Washington, D.C. police force had made significant strides in recruiting minority applicants. Significantly, even though the Court technically was not interpreting Title VII or the EEOC *Guidelines*, the majority decision went out of its way to indicate that the job-relatedness requirement of Title VII, if applicable, would not have been interpreted to require a different result: "Nor is the conclusion foreclosed by either *Griggs* or *Albemarle Company v. Moody*, 422 U.S. 405 (1975); and it seems to us the much more sensible construction of the job-relatedness requirement." *Id.* at 250-51.

25. United States v. South Carolina, 445 F. Supp. 1094 (D.S.C. 1977), *aff'd* 434 U.S. 1026 (1978). In order to validate the NTE for local certification purposes, ETS had assembled local educators in South Carolina who opined that the content of the NTE, which was created to test knowledge of subject matter taught in teacher training institutions nationwide, reflected the particular curriculum being taught in the teacher training institutions in that state. 445 F. Supp. at 1112. Plaintiffs argued that the job-relatedness requirements of the EEOC *Guidelines* required not a correlation with training course content, but a correlation with the skills and knowledge needed for effective performance as a classroom teacher on the job. *See id.* at 1108 n. 13. The three-judge panel, relying on *Davis*, upheld the training course validation. Justice White, the author of the *Davis* opinion, strongly dissented from the Supreme Court's summary affirmance:

> . . .*Washington v. Davis*, in this respect, held only that the test. . . which sought to ascertain whether the applicant had the minimum communication skills necessary to understand the offerings in a police training course, could be used to measure eligibility to enter that program. The case did not hold that a training course, the completion of which is required for employment, need not itself be validated in terms of job-relatedness. Nor did it hold that a test that a job applicant must pass and that is designed to indicate his mastery of the materials or skills taught in the training course, can be validated without reference to the job.

434 U.S. at 1027.

26. *See generally*, Shimberg, *Testing for Licensure and Certification*, 36 AM. PSYCHOLOGIST 1138 (1981); Dent v. West Virginia, 129 U.S. 114, 122 (1889) ("The nature and extent of the qualifications required of doctors must depend primarily upon the judgment of the State as to their necessity.");

Douglas v. Noble, 261 U.S. 165 (1923) (States may delegate broad authority to administrative agencies to examine the qualifications of dentists); Smith v. California, 336 F.2d 530, 534 (9th Cir. 1964) ("The principles stated in the Dent case have been widely applied by all the States in a great variety of professions. . ."); Goldfarb v. Virginia State Bar, 421 U.S. 773, 792 (1975) (". . .the States. . .have broad power to establish standards for licensing practitioners and regulating the practice of professions.")

27.   474 F. Supp. 244 (M.D. Fla. 1979), *aff'd in part and vacated in part,* 644 F.2d 397 (5th Cir. 1981), *on remand* 564 F. Supp. 177 (M.D. Fla. 1983), *aff'd* 730 F.2d 1405 (11th Cir. 1984).

28.   730 F.2d at 1407-09.

29.   Thirty-seven states have enacted minimum competency legislation. Logar, *Minimum Competency Testing in Schools: Legislative Action and Judicial Review,* 13 J. OF LAW & ED. 35, 38 (1984). For a detailed overview of the range of minimum competency programs, *see* W. P. GORTH, A STUDY OF MINIMUM COMPETENCY TESTING PROGRAMS (ERIC II ED 185, 123 1979).

30.   *See, e.g.,* McClung, *Competency Testing Programs: Legal and Educational Issues,* 47 FORDHAM L. REV. 651, 687-98 (1979). The support for student competency testing, like that for teacher competency testing, has resulted from a complex coalition of political forces. Many conservatives have strongly favored student competency testing because they believe that emphasis on basic-skill tests will foster a return to traditional pedagogical methods. At the same time, many liberal educational reformers, including some minority group spokespersons, have also strongly supported MCT in the belief that dramatizing the degree of instructional failure of the schools will build support for more innovative educational approaches. This contrast between conservative and liberal expectations demonstrates the ambiguity of the assumptions of the MCT movement: widespread test failures may be read as indications of either student or school system incompetence. For useful discussions of the competency testing movement, see McClung, *supra;* Lerner, *The Minimum Competence Movement: Social, Scientific and Legal Implications* 36 AM. PSYCHOLOGIST 1057 (1981); Haney and Madaus, *Making Sense of the Competency Testing Movement,* 48 HARV. EDUC. REV. 462 (1978).

31.   *Debra P.,* 474 F. Supp. 244, 248 (M.D. Fla. 1979).

32.   Specifically, the Court stated that the test had adequate content and construct validity. *Id.* at 261. Although technically Title VII and the EEOC *Guidelines* did not apply to the student competency testing sector, the test validation concepts that had been extensively developed in the employment discrimination area were indirectly brought into the case through claims based on allegations of discrimination under Title VI of the 1964 Civil Rights Act and the 14th Amendment.

33.   474 F. Supp. at 254.

34. *Id.*

35. *Id.* at 269.

36. The Court used the term "curricular validity," but the concept it had in mind clearly was closer to "instructional validity." McClung, an attorney for the plaintiffs in *Debra P.*, apparently was the first to discuss these concepts extensively. He defined "instructional validity" as a measure of "whether or not the school district's stated objectives were translated into topics and actually taught in the district's classrooms." By way of contrast, the term "curriculum validity," as defined by McClung, represented a "measure of how well test items represent the objectives of the curriculum to which the test takers have been exposed." *See* McClung, *Competency Testing: Potential for Discrimination*, CLEARINGHOUSE REV. 439, 446 (Sept. 1977). In order to avoid confusion in terms, the validation requirement articulated by the Court in *Debra P.* will be referred to throughout this article as "instructional validity."

37. 664 F.2d at 405.

38. Standard 8.7 of the newly adopted *Standards for Educational and Psychological Testing, supra* note 17, states:

> When a test is used to make decisions about student promotion and graduation, there should be evidence that the test covers only the specific or generalized knowledge, skills, and abilities that the students have had the opportunity to learn.

39. *See, e.g.,* Note, *Testing the Tests: The Due Process Implications of Minimum Competency Testing,* 59 N.Y.U. L. REV. 577 (1984); GARCIA, *supra* note 4, at 62ff.

40. To be fully equitable, an additional showing of how well each individual child was taught, and how much or how recently, might also be required. *See, e.g.,* Debra P. v. Turlington, 654 F.2d 1079, 1083 (on petition for rehearing en banc, Tjoflat, J., dissenting).

41. Methods proposed for accomplishing this include techniques for classroom observations, teacher self-reports, student self-reports, and development of individual pupil cumulative record cards. These issues are discussed generally in the articles collected in THE COURTS, VALIDITY AND COMPETENCY TESTING (G. Madaus ed. 1983). *See also,* McClung, *supra* note 30, at 705-08.

42. R. VENESKY, *Curricular Validity: The Case for Structure and Process,* in Madaus, *supra* at 183, 193.

43. 564 F. Supp. at 184. *See also* Anderson v. Banks, 540 F. Supp. 761, 765-66 (S.D. Ga. 1982) (". . .to require school officials to produce testimony that every teacher finished every lesson and assigned every problem in the curriculum would impose a paralyzing burden on school authorities. . .").

44.   As indicated *supra* note 36, although the Fifth Circuit's 1981 decision had used the term "curricular validity," it clearly meant to impose a requirement synonymous with "instructional validity" since it required a showing that test objectives "covered things actually taught in the classrooms." The court's confusion about the terms is in itself an indication of the conceptual complexities involved.

45.   564 F. Supp. at 186.

46.   730 F.2d at 1412. This results from the fact that "instructional validity" is an argument for adequate test preparation, and strictly speaking, ". . .it is not a form of validity at all." Yalow & Popham, *Content Validity at the Crossroads*, 12 EDUC. RESEARCHER 10, 12 (1983).

47.   This impression is further substantiated by the fact that in all other Eleventh Circuit decisions invoking *Debra P.*, the court found grounds on which to distinguish it and avoided applying the instructional validation doctrine. *See* Bester v. Tuscaloosa City Board of Education, 722 F.2d 1514 (11th Cir. 1984) (plaintiffs held to lack a property right in expectation of promotion despite standard reading test scores); Love v. Turlington, 733 F.2d 1562 (11th Cir. 1984) (Florida's basic skills test for eleventh graders involves diploma sanction and therefore does not meet typical requirements for class certification). *See also* Anderson v. Banks, 520 F. Supp. 472, 509 (S.D. Ga. 1981) (*Debra P.* concept questioned but applied); 540 F. Supp. 761 (S.D. Ga. 1982), *appeal dismissed on other grounds sub. nom.* Johnson v. Sikes, 730 F.2d 644 (11th Cir. 1984) ("curricular validity" upheld on the basis of educational authority's general testimony; empirical field evidence considered impractical); Brookhart v. Illinois State Board of Education, 697 F.2d 179 (7th Cir. 1982); Board of Education of Northport-East Northport Union Free School District v. Ambach, 60 N.Y.2d 758 (1983) (handicapped students denied diplomas for failure to pass minimum competency tests covering areas not included in their individualized education programs).

48.   Thus, the complaint in Allen v. Alabama State Board of Education, 612 F. Supp. 1046 (M.D. Ala. 1985), *vacated* Feb. 4, 1986, alleged, *inter alia*, "[T]hat said tests covered materials much of which was not taught students in Alabama's colleges and universities, particularly the predominantly black state and private colleges and universities in Alabama." *Id.* Para. 17b. *See also*, Center for Educational Testing and Evaluation, *Report on the Validation Studies of the National Teacher Examinations*, University of Kansas (1985) (Extensive curricular validity and instructional validity studies applied to teacher certification tests).

49.   *See* United States v. Lulac, F.2d (5th Cir, July 2, 1986). Note, *Minimum Competency Testing of Teachers for Certification*, *supra* note 19, listed a number of other arguments for distinguishing the student testing situation in *Debra P.* from the teacher certification as follows:

> First, enrollment in teacher training programs is not compulsory, unlike school attendance for children. Second, attendance in teacher training programs is relatively short term compared to the twelve years of attendance required for receipt of a high school diploma.

> Third, failure to obtain teacher certification does not preclude most other forms of gainful employment, unlike possession of a high school diploma, which today is a prerequisite to many forms of gainful employment

Id. at 502.

The Supreme Court upheld validation based on the local teacher training college curriculum in the United States v. South Carolina, 434 U.S. 1026 (1978), *supra* note 25, but did so on a record which offered as the sole alternative to objective testing a discretionary approval procedure that the Court considered highly undesirable. *See*, 445 F. Supp. at 1115-1116. If the psychometric profession can now provide a job-related certification examination as an acceptable alternative, courts should endorse this preferred approach. In this context, *South Carolina* would not provide precedent for adding an additional, and inconsistent, instructional validation requirement to an otherwise acceptable job-related examination. *Cf.* Ensley Branch of NAACP V. Seibels, 616 F.2d 812, 819, n.17 (5th Cir. 1980), *cert. denied* 449 U.S. 1061 (training program validation suitable only for tests of minimum reading and verbal skills).

50. Judge Justice recently referred to *Debra P.* in partially granting plaintiffs' motion for a preliminary injunction to limit the use of the Texas Pre-Professional Skills Test (P-PST) for entry into teacher preparation program, holding that the State must demonstrate 'that students in Texas had been taught the materials covered in the P-PST' *United States v. State of Texas*, 628 F. Supp. 304, 320 (E.D. Tex). This decision was, however, reversed by the Fifth Circuit, in a decision which strongly emphasized the state's "interest in ensuring teacher competency" [p. 7012]. The Appeals Court held that a preliminary injunction should not be issued before there has been a full trial on the merits of the complex test validation issues raised by the case. Speaking directly to the public policy concerns being discussed in this article, the Court also stated, "In administering its higher education systems, even a state that formerly practiced *de jure* segregation has no constitutional or statutory obligation to suspend or lower valid academic standards to accommodate high school students who may be ill prepared because of prior constitutional violations by its local and elementary school systems." [p. 7015].

51. "[N]othing in these guidelines is intended or should be interpreted as discouraging the use of a selection procedure for the purpose of determining qualifications or for the purpose of selection on the basis of relative qualifications, if the selection procedure has been validated in accord with these guidelines for each such purpose for which it is to be used." 29 C.F.R. § 1607.2(c).

52. 29 C.F.R. § 1607.3 (b)

53. *See, e.g.*, REPORT OF THE COMMITTEE ON ABILITY TESTING, NATIONAL RESEARCH COUNCIL, ABILITY TESTING: USES, CONSEQUENCES, AND CONTROVERSIES AT 18 (1982) ("certain social groups tend, as groups, to score consistently lower on the average than more advantaged groups. . .."); Clady v. County of Los Angeles, 770 F.2d 1421, 1432-33 (9th Cir. 1985) (court rejects appelants' contention that they

met "the virtually impossible burden of identifying alternative selection devices which satisfy the employer's legitimate hiring needs.") *See also*, Rivera v. City of Wichita Falls, 665 F.2d 531, 538 (5th Cir. 1982).

54. *Golden Rule Insurance Company v. Washburn*, Consent Decree, No. 419-76, Ill. Circ. Ct. 7th Jud. Circ., Nov. 20, 1984.

55. Cordes, *ETS to Reweigh Test Items' Racial Bias*, APA Monitor, Feb. 1985, at 26.

56. Golden Rule Insurance Company v. Washburn, Consent Decree of Nov. 20, 1984, Para. 6(a).

57. *Id.* at Para. 6(b).

58. *See* Cordes, *supra* note 55 at 26 (comments of Prof. Robert Linn raising blueprint issues).

59. *See, e.g.,* Hoover, *The Reliability of Six Item Bias Indices*, 8 APPLIED PSYCHOLOGICAL MEASUREMENT 173, 180 (1984). Note also that the item bias approach, by eliminating the use of certain items, requires a larger item pool, thereby increasing test construction costs. The National Council on Measurement in Education recently stated in letters opposing legislation that would mandate utilization of "Golden Rule" techniques in New York and California that:

> These bills would result in severe adverse consequences for those individuals and educational institutions that objective tests are designed to serve. We have studied the most recent drafts of these pieces of legislation carefully. They are based on the erroneous assumption that differences in the proportions of students in various groups that answer test items correctly provide evidence that test items are biased against members of these groups. These bills are also based on the assumption that items showing group performance differences of more than 15% and items that cannot be answered correctly by more than 40% of minority students, so-called "Type II" items, are "biased" against members of the lower scoring group and should be preferentially avoided in test construction. Both of these assumptions are seriously flawed. They do not correspond to measurement specialists' understanding of the meaning of group performance differences and do not lead to acceptable professional practice in test development and use.

Letter from Richard M. Jaeger, President, National Council on Measurement in Education, to New York State Senator Arthur Eve (Apr. 29, 1986) (on file with YALE LAW & POLICY REVIEW). *See also* letter from Richard M. Jaeger to California State Senator Gary Hart (Apr. 29, 1986) (on file with YALE LAW & POLICY REVIEW).

60. *Insurance Agent Tests Face Change to Settle Suit*, Wall St. J., Nov. 29, 1984, at 3. ETS' news release on the day of the settlement explained its motivations for settling as follows:

"We are confident the examination would have withstood the scrutiny of the courts," said Stanford von Mayrhauser, general counsel of ETS, the non-profit organization which developed the test. "The lawsuit was dismissed twice by the courts in the eight years since the case began. The settlement found no fault with the test. We are not required to change the content of the examination but we may make such changes as we see fit. ETS will not pay any damages to the plaintiffs or any of the plaintiffs' costs," von Mayrhauser added. "In light of the favorable agreement reached, we saw no good reason to devote large amounts of time, energy, and money to continue the litigation."

61.   *Test Service Accepts Safeguards Against Bias*, N.Y. Times, Nov. 29, 1984, at B17.

62.   *Id.*

63.   Allen v. Alabama State Board of Education, 612 F. Supp. 1046 (M.D. Ala. 1985), Consent decree, July 12, 1985.

64.   This decree has had an unusual history and its final status is still unclear. Immediately after counsel for the State Education Department had agreed to the consent decree, the Attorney General objected both to its substance (among other things, it required the state to certify 500 members of the class who had failed the examination and to pay $500,000 in liquidated damages) and to counsel's authority to bind the state to settle. Counsel's consent was based on the position of the State Commissioner of Education, and on the lack of opposition from members of the State Board of Education when the proposed settlement had been discussed with them.

After the Attorney General publicized his objections, the members of the State Board of Education formally met and officially voted to reject the consent decree. Although initially ruling that their prior actions constituted an approval which was now binding, Allen v. Alabama State Board of Education, 612 F. Supp. 1046, 1052 (M.D. Ala. 1985), the Court, upon rehearing, held that in light of the broad public policy issues involved, it would vacate the settlement order and not impose the controversial consent decree on the now clearly unwilling defendants. The Court also certified the questions for immediate appeal. Allen v. Alabama, Civ. No. 81-697, Order of Feb. 4, 1986. That appeal is pending, as are the results of the trial which concluded in June, 1986. (The author is representing NES, the test developer, as *amicus curiae* at the trial.) Both on appeal and at trial, the issues involving the item bias techniques set forth in the original settlement are likely to receive substantial attention.

65.   Allen v. Alabama, Consent Decree of July 12, 1985, Para. 2(b)-(d).

66.   There is, however, a way in which the statistical techniques utilized in *Golden Rule* could be used to assist in minimizing any true bias without undermining the tests' basic integrity. Statistical indications of disparities in the performance of different racial groups (especially as reflected in the more sophisticated form of item bias analysis known as item response

theory, which differentiates black and white test takers of equal achievement levels rather than gross group statistics) can be used to "flag" items which need to be reconsidered by an expert review panel. *See generally*, HANDBOOK OF METHODS FOR DETECTING TEST BIAS (R. A. Berk ed. 1982). Such a panel of knowledgeable persons (including a significant proportion of minority representatives) should carefully review the particular question to determine whether the cause of the statistical disparities is cultural bias in the wording of the question, or a deficiency in the educational preparation of the subject group of test takers, or other factors. If cultural bias does exist, the item clearly should be reworded or eliminated. If biased phrasing or content cannot be articulated, however, the item should be retained so that the test's integrity is not compromised.

67.   Gifford, *We Must Interrupt the Cycle of Minority Group Failure*, Education Week, Mar. 20, 1985, at 24.

68.   Maeroff, *Leader of Education Association Backs Testing for New Teachers*, N.Y. Times, July 1, 1985, at A13, col 3.

69.   Recent data on rising achievement test scores of minority applicants provide empirical support for the proposition that minority teacher candidates will fare better on the exams as their educational opportunities improve. For example, between 1976 and 1984, mean scores of black students on the Scholastic Aptitude Test (SAT) rose 10 points on the verbal part of the test and 19 on the mathematical, and mean score differences on the SAT between all students and black students were reduced by 13 percent on the verbal portion and 18 percent on the mathematical. Similarly, reading scores of black students tested at ages 9, 13, and 17 improved steadily and consistently between 1970 and 1980. Anrig, *Educational Standards, Testing, and Equity*, PHI DELTA KAPPAN, May 1985, at 624.

70.   Professor William Mehrens, past President of the National Council on Measurement in Education, has aptly stated the core issue as follows:

> The solution to the problem of incompetent teachers be they black or white is to work at increasing their competence, not allowing them to teach in spite of their incompetence due to sympathy, guilt, or some perversion of the notion of justice.

Mehrens, *supra* note 13 at 70.

71.   These recommendations are set forth as suggestions for further analysis. No claim is made that a definitive legal basis for enforcing them presently exists. The proposals are geared to the circumstances of entry-level teacher candidates who are denied initial certification. The extent to which the situation of incumbent teachers, who in some states may be denied certification renewal if they fail a competency test, differs from that of entry-level candidates is not discussed in this article.

72.   Specific diagnostic information concerning each student's strengths and weaknesses should be provided to all candidates after administration of each test.

73. Such disclosure is required by canons of fairness and would not necessarily discourage all applicants from applying to the school, especially if it offered other academic benefits. For example, many law schools with strong national reputations do not purport to prepare their graduates for any particular bar examination; graduates of these schools generally assume that they will need to take an intensive short-term course on state law and procedures before sitting for a state bar examination.

74. Debra P. v. Turlington, 474 F. Supp. at 269.

75. The district court also found that the State had denied the students due process by giving them little notice of, and no materials on, the nature of the tests, other than a pamphlet. While an individual is entitled to notice and a hearing before state action deprives him of life, liberty, or property, no such right attends legislative enactments that affect general class of persons. When the legislature enacts a law, or a state agency adopts a regulation, that affects a general class of persons, all of those persons have received procedural due process by the legislative process itself and they have no right to individual attention. *United States v. Lulac, supra.* n.49 at [p. 7014].

76. *See, e.g.,* Ayres, *Student Achievement at Predominantly White and Predominantly Black Universities,* 20 AM. EDUC. RESEARCH J. 291 (1983) (controlling for SAT scores, blacks attending predominantly white institutions averaged twenty-five points higher on NTE commons than blacks attending predominantly black institutions); *Black Colleges Lag on Georgia Teacher Test,* Atlanta Journal, Jan. 14, 1985, at A1, A9.

77. *See, e.g.,* United States v. State of Alabama, Civ. No. 83-C-1676-S(N.D. Ala. Dec. 7, 1985) (findings that dual system of higher education still exists in Alabama).

78. *Id.* Judge Clemon indicated that black students who attend many of the predominantly white institutions appear to be well integrated into campus life.

79. What is needed is a concerted campaign to attract larger numbers of academically talented black students into the teaching profession and to restructure the education departments at historically black colleges. The competency testing and certification examinations that some consider necessary evils may reveal some of the difficulties of minority students and help them better prepare for the future. Dilworth, *Teachers Totter: A Report on Teacher Certification Issues* at 39 (Occasional paper of The Institute for the Study of Educational Policy No. 6, Howard University, 1984).

80. Gifford, *supra,* note 67, at 24. *Compare* Smith, *supra* note 7. Smith supports eliminating standardized certification tests and proposes affirmative action teacher recruitment programs.

81. *See, e.g.,* M. REBELL & A. BLOCK, EDUCATIONAL POLICY MAKING AND THE COURTS (1982).

82.   The examples discussed in this article reflect a broader phenomenon that has marked the entire development of Title VII test validation doctrine. The original EEOC *Guidelines* incorporated evolving concepts of test validation proposed by a section of the American Psychological Association. The Supreme Court's decision in *Griggs*, 401 U.S. 424 (1971), gave these procedures a supervening legitimacy. Within psychometric circles, the EEOC *Guidelines* became the incontrovertible core of professional standards. An analogous process has taken place in the area of I.Q. tests for student classification purposes. *See* Larry P. v. Riles, 495 F. Supp. 926 (N.D. Cal. 1979), *aff'd* No. 80-4027 (9th Cir. Jan. 23, 1984); Prasse and Reschly, *Larry P.: A Case of Segregation, Testing, or Program Efficacy?*, 52 EXCEPTIONAL CHILDREN 333 (1986); Bersoff, *Regarding Psychologists Testily: Legal Regulation of Psychological Assessment in the Public Schools*, 39 MD. L. REV. 27 (1979); *cf.* Pase v. Hannan, 506 F. Supp. 831 (N.D. Ill. 1980). *See also*, D. STONE, THE DISABLED STATE (1984) (comparative analysis of judicial and medical determinations of disability for welfare benefit programs).

Professional Testing for Teachers

Albert Shanker

A Mood of Reform

The testing of prospective teachers is one of the most important issues in education today. To understand its significance fully, however, it is useful to do a quick run-through of the recent education reform movement.

We have been through a three-year wave of reform, and many people are surprised that reform sentiments continue. Yet new reports keep coming out and legislators are still concerned. This reform movement is not the result of a Sputnik or a baby boom; that is, some external challenge. The reform movement this time came as a result of a rather mature understanding, mainly by the business community but also by the political community, of certain realities. The investment in rebuilding our physical infrastructure, our industries, or our military capability would not be successful unless there were parallel investments in the human infrastructure.

Today's concern with education parallels our approach to the energy crisis. While we do not face the shortages of 1973-1974, we all know that we still must be concerned about conservation. And even if we are relieved that oil prices are low right now, we have retained that consciousness of concern. It is an understanding that is very different from the flashes of public interest that often afflict us. In education, too, the public is not only aware of the need for reform, but also, in state after state, has approved tax increases for education. Unfortunately, the public often expects results overnight; this is not likely to happen.

A RETURN TO BASICS

The current reformers are asking us to take the schools back to where they were in 1950; that is, have a core curriculum, test teachers before they enter the classroom, do not promote students automatically, etc. Given the schools of 1950 and the schools of 1975, I would prefer the schools of 1950. I prefer a system that is tighter, that has requirements and expectations, and in which everyone does not automatically succeed as a result of merely attending.

Albert Shanker is President of the American Federation of Teachers.

Unfortunately, the system of 1950 is not one that now serves our country well. What percentage of the students in 1950 graduated, and how many dropped out? How many went into vocational or general programs that simply stored them for a while? The fact is that we retained and graduated fewer students then than we do now, largely because we turned our backs on minorities and also ignored hard-to-educate youngsters.

We have today heightened expectations to match our greater needs. For example, when the first person retired on Social Security, 15 people were in the workforce to support that person. By 1996, for every person depending on Social Security, there will be three adults in the workforce, and one of those three will be black or Hispanic. If we do not do a better job of reaching blacks, Hispanics, and those whites who are not making it, we may very well have an America in which for every two people who are working, one is supporting a person on Social Security and the other is supporting someone on welfare. That signifies an economic situation with a drastically reduced standard of living from what we enjoy now. A change of that magnitude threatens the entire fabric of society.

PUBLIC SCHOOLING

We are also at a point in history when people are asking whether public education will continue to be the major delivery system of education. This is a more open question than it has been through most of our history. About 50 percent of the American people now believe that the government ought to subsidize (through tax breaks and vouchers) their right to take their children out of public schools and find other alternatives. The decision on this issue will not hang on general arguments over whether public education is worth maintaining. I have met quite a few parents who philosophically believe in public education but do not want to "sacrifice" their own children. The issue will be resolved on whether the quality of public education can be improved sufficiently so that it is satisfactory to a well-educated public with high expectations. And the key to that is attracting and retaining a high-quality teaching force into our nation's schools.

We all know what that involves, even though we don't act on it: better salaries and a real professional environment for teaching. But less well understood is the role of tests in professionalizing teaching and making it a more attractive profession. Current tests simply don't fit the bill.

Testing Teachers

This chapter will return to the relationship of testing to these issues, but I would like now to focus on the topic of what teacher certification tests should measure, what makes for a valid measurement instrument. As the program of a recent testing company-sponsored conference noted, "Validity is a multifaceted concept. It entails legal and technical concerns as well as educational issues." I think that sentence indicates the order of priority many, including most in the testing industry, place on testing. The order of the statement is symptomatic of the current condition and mentality in teacher testing. It emphasizes testing as a technical, legal, and bureaucratic concern. The educational issues enter at the very end. In discussions in recent years on testing issues, people seem primarily concerned with: Will the test stand up in the courts? Will the states or districts buy it? How much does it cost? The issue of what kinds of teachers do we want, or need, to attract and retain in our school is never engaged.

EMPHASIS ON THE TECHNICAL

The fanatic is one who redoubles his efforts after he has forgotten his aims. In testing, we have been redoubling our efforts with an eye only toward technical and legal concerns without bothering to look at what we may be trying to accomplish in education.

Testing of prospective teachers is purely instrumental, a matter of sorting and screening, where to set the cutoff score, how to prove job relatedness, which test items to delete on the basis of a field test, and the like. It is this focus that gives testing, and eventually teachers, a bad name, because sooner or later a researcher comes along with a study that shows that doing well on these tests has nothing to do with good professional practice. That should be no surprise. Today's tests have little to do with substance and are driven mainly by procedural and technical concerns.

A HIGHER FUNCTION

There is another function for tests, and that is rarely mentioned in the discussions of testing. It is a function that does exist in other professions. That purpose is the role of tests in defining the professional knowledge base. What is worth knowing ought to be the first question in developing a test.

Candidates for, say, a bar exam or an exam in medicine or architecture, know what they have to study. They know the

knowledge domains that they must master. They know what and
how they are going to have to demonstrate that knowledge. Those
exams reflect a standard of professional knowledge that does not
fluctuate with passing rates or cutoff scores. A truly professional
test, in contrast to teacher tests, is driven by the *relevance* of the
knowledge rather than by the *reliability* of the individual test items,
by the *value* of the knowledge and the knowledge domain in
professional practice rather than by the job *validation* procedure.

CONTENT TESTS

One can argue, of course, that the current teacher tests do reflect
a standard of knowledge. But let us look at what these tests say
about what a teacher ought to know. If we take a subject-matter
test, for example, the National Teacher Examinations (NTE), we
find it is based on what a college major in that subject ought to
know. But the NTE tests leave off at factual recall; few underlying
concepts are ever engaged. Other tests, such as those constructed
by National Evaluation Systems, Inc., are based on the content of
the school curriculum, which means that teachers need know only
what they will be asked to teach at the grade level they will be
teaching. If one will teach high school math, then one need know
only high school math.

But what of the structure involved in mathematics, the ways of
conveying that structure to different kinds of students? What of
the students who will not understand it when the teacher has
presented it one way, and for whom the teacher may have to
present it in a second way, and a third way, a fourth, and fifth
way? Each of these other ways may involve a level of understanding
of mathematics that is considerably above and beyond what the
students are supposed to know.

TESTS OF PEDAGOGY

The situation with tests of pedagogy is even worse. In what other
profession does one routinely have untrained people, usually
newspaper reporters, sitting for an examination and passing it
easily as a part of an "experiment"? What other profession uses
tests that contain one sentence, context-free questions, with four
or five proposed multiple-choice answers, two or three of which
may be correct, depending on the situation? Anyone who knows
anything about education would answer most of these questions
with "It all depends."

Current tests of pedagogy measure knowledge of context-free
techniques, the ability to read, and test-taking skills. Instead, there

ought to be ways for these tests, like other professional tests, to allow candidates to demonstrate judgment and the ability to deal with context and contingencies. That is what teaching, like other professions, is all about. No multiple-choice test, which is all we have, can do that.

In fact, this approach can lead to real problems. For example, on Florida's "research-based" test, one is forced to choose one side of the research evidence, again, with no context. The answers in the Florida tests presume that whole-class instruction is the right approach to teaching. If one doesn't work from that perspective, one will have great difficulties on that test. Obviously, the test itself does not state its assumptions. On the other hand, the NTE has a clear bias toward individualized instruction. Doing well on the Florida test may mean doing poorly on the NTE, unless one knows in advance the assumptions that underlie each, which is a test-taking skill. Thus the tests do not really reflect the knowledge base of professional education or even skill in pedagogy.

The Case for a Professional Test

It does not have to be this way. Other professions have figured out ways of incorporating context, uncertainty, and judgment. We have looked too little at how professional examinations operate in other fields.

BAR EXAMS

For example, the bar examination uses case approaches, in which candidates are given a variety of materials necessary for developing a brief. They must organize the materials into a coherent, defensible argument. Also, bar examinations use essays, so that the candidates are able to display knowledge of the issues, precedents, and cases and can bring much of themselves to their answers. The tests have no absolutely right answers; many applicants will answer in very different ways or will reach different conclusions. The important issue is how candidates reach their conclusions and whether the process is professional and acceptable. A lawyer, looking at the reasoning, would say that this or that person can practice side by side with us because he or she engages in the same type of thinking, arguing, and intelligence gathering that is necessary to function successfully in law.

OTHER AREAS

In medicine, examinations use simulations of cases on computers, with the presentation of information and an interactive questioning mode. In psychiatry, simulations with real patients, one-way mirrors, and a jury of psychiatrists observing the candidate interviewing a patient are a part of professional assessment. The point, again, is not the right diagnosis but the appropriateness of the questions and interactions that are used to elicit the information and to arrive at a diagnosis. The candidate is also interviewed by the jury observers and has an opportunity to explain why he or she took a given approach.

The Role of the Profession

Why do other professional examinations evidence this level of sophistication, this respect for knowledge and the role of uncertainty and judgment? Why are these exams professional while teacher exams look more like those for a driver's license? Chief among the reasons is that other professional exams are controlled by the profession. The development of the exam may be contracted out, but the client is the profession itself. It is this kind of professional control that would lead to the definition of the knowledge base in teaching and to the further professionalization of teaching.

Right now the tests accurately reflect what teaching is: a bureaucratic occupation, a technical enterprise. The largest single category of questions on the NTE, for instance, has to do with appropriate bureaucratic behaviors, not the ability to put knowledge into practice. For example, there is a question that states, more or less:

> What do you do if a group comes to you and complains about the textbook you are using?
>
> A.   Refer them to school board policy.
> B.   Talk to the principal about it.
> C.   Ask them if they can suggest something better to use.
> D.   Claim First Amendment rights to determine what to teach.

The correct answer on the NTE is C, although why is not clear to me. Basically, the correct answer is the one that creates the least problem for central administration. The test also asks about the ethics of taking a second job when you are a teacher, student obscenity, paperwork routines, and so forth.

In Georgia, for another example, doing well on the part of the test that examines the administrative aspects of teaching is important for passing the test and being certified. Unfortunately, some research shows that tending well to administrative features of teaching, such as paperwork routines and planning around behavioral objectives, has substantial negative correlation with student achievement. The resulting problems are apparent.

THE PROFESSION AS CLIENT

So long as the bureaucracy and not the profession is the client of the test, this situation will continue. There is currently no professional client in teacher testing. To be sure, the testing companies enlist advisory committees, and there is teacher input, and all the "right" political actors are at the table. Despite the input, there appears to be no control over the body of knowledge that represents the profession. Similarly, to the extent that the teaching profession has control over cutoff (passing) scores, it is only through a so-called validation process that has teachers and teacher educators commenting on whether an item is easy or hard or whether or not it is covered in their work. So long as teachers are adjuncts to this testing process rather than its clients, so long as test developers rather than the teaching profession develop the body of knowledge that defines teaching and make decisions about content and standards, teacher tests will continue to be a subject of ridicule, and the people who pass them will gain little more respect than those who do not.

KNOWLEDGE BASE

With all due respect to the test developers, I do not think that you will solve this problem, and I also believe that you have inadvertently contributed to the debasement of teaching by attempting to define the knowledge base in education, a task that rightly falls to teachers themselves. The key issue here is that of the knowledge base. If there is no knowledge base, obviously there is nothing to test except subject matter. If there is a knowledge base, it needs to be assembled and it should assert that there are defensible answers on issues of professional knowledge.

Admittedly, we in education do not have a very good history in this respect. Most principals or superintendents, if challenged about doing things in a certain way—using a certain textbook, urging a certain curriculum—would respond, "It is all a matter of opinion; nobody really knows anything for sure." This is a ridiculous defense, because if nobody knows anything, why should we be certified to teach in the first place? One cannot defend public investments and a credentialing system unless teaching requires something that nobody else has. Defining that content and finding individuals who possess that knowledge is the job of a test for teacher certification.

Directions for Teacher Testing

I would like to close this chapter with a number of suggestions about testing that I think are necessary if we are to get on the right track.

A NATIONAL EXAMINATION

Almost two years ago, I suggested a national teacher examination to replace the varied state examinations and offerings from private companies. It is critical that the examination be based on the work of the outstanding minds of the country as to what the knowledge base for education is, as well as subject-matter knowledge. The purchaser of the test should be a national board of professional educators, not individual states or districts. The national board should comprise a group of outstanding and knowledgeable practitioners, and it should be independent of government or other political control.

Currently, individual states are developing their own examinations. Each of those states is likely to duplicate, at least in part, what exists. The result is twenty or thirty states, each with its own version of the same thing. Besides being counterintuitive, it exacerbates the mobility problem for teachers. One does not have to become a doctor or a pharmacist all over again when one moves from state to state. But a teacher who moves is likely to be required to take education courses and another examination, as well as give up his or her salary base and pension. The reason a lot of people "used to be" teachers is that people are not about to start all over again every time they move somewhere. We need to say to the public that a teacher may move from one place to another without having to requalify and without sacrificing earned benefits. A national instrument will contribute to this solution.

INTERNSHIPS

Any examination must be connected to an internship or residency program because you cannot find out if a person is going to be a good teacher solely on the basis of test results. It is true that one can find out if a candidate is illiterate or lacking in content knowledge, and those are very important pieces of information. If a person is illiterate, I do not care what warm or caring qualities he or she has; that person should not teach. So the written parts of the examination are necessary, but not sufficient, indicators of teaching potential.

Part of an examining system should be an internship. Teaching is the only field where one is given the same responsibilities on the first day of employment in the profession as one will have thirty years later. I believe that idealistic and knowledgeable teachers come into a classroom with all sorts of ideas about what they are going to do. They are immediately faced with the problem of how to defend themselves and how to control the students; the result is the abandonment of many learned teaching techniques. And yet we do not devise training programs that confront this issue realistically. An internship period under the guidance of experienced teachers would be invaluable in helping new teachers through that difficult first period. A number of state and national education reform reports have now recommended internships.

Conclusion

Let me return to the very beginning, then: the future of the education reform movement and public education itself. The importance of how these issues are resolved cannot be overestimated. At the same time, as the public has developed high expectations and political figures have invested additional dollars for education, what is likely to happen is that states will spend more and more money to get teachers, but the teachers are likely to be less qualified.

The reason for this is, in large part, that some traditionally male professions are becoming increasingly open to women. These would include accounting, advertising, banking and finance, business and management, computer information sciences, data processing, engineering, journalism, law, medicine, personnel management, and pharmacy. In each the percentage of women who got bachelor's and master's and professional degrees in these fields increased dramatically between 1973 and 1983. In some the majority of degrees were earned by women.

What we do during this reform period is key to whether the public decides to continue investing in public education or selects alternatives. Teachers who will enter the classroom in the immediate future include many who are barely literate and for whom we are paying more and more money. The result is a school system that looks worse, and will be worse, than it was 10 or 15 years ago, and there is dynamite in this, and it will explode public education.

We have to devise tests that make people proud to be entering the field because they are being asked to do something that challenges them, that is of value, and that is close to the heart of what they will be doing as professionals. At stake is nothing less than the future of public education.

The Validity Issue in Texas

Marvin Veselka

In the late 1970s, Texas was not unique among states in its concern for improvements in teacher preparation, school curriculum, and other educational areas. The Advisory Committee on Education under Governor William P. Clements, Jr., made a number of significant recommendations which were to be implemented over the next several years. This was in 1979, four years before the Select Committee on Public Education, chaired by H. Ross Perot, began its work. The Select Committee, appointed by Governor Mark White, received national attention for its reform posture.

Even before the Select Committee started its review of public education in the state, Texas undertook a number of major reforms. Two of these reforms were in the areas of teacher certification testing and public school curriculum. Legislation passed in 1981 stated:

> . . .the [State Board of Education] by rule shall require satisfactory performance after graduation from an in-state or out-of-state teacher education program on a comprehensive examination prescribed by the board as a condition to full certification as a teacher and shall require satisfactory performance on a separate examination prescribed by the board as a condition to certification as a superintendent or other administrator. The board shall prescribe an examination designed to test knowledge appropriate for certification to teach primary grades and an examination designed to test knowledge appropriate for certification to teach secondary grades. The secondary teacher examinations must test knowledge of each examinee in the subject areas listed. . . .

Additional legislation at the same time called for each school district to offer

> . . .a well-balanced curriculum that includes: (1) English Language Arts; (2) other languages, to the extent possible; (3) mathematics; (4) science; (5) health; (6) physical education; (7) fine arts; (8) social studies; (9) economics, with emphasis on the free enterprise system and its benefits; (10) business education; (11) vocational education; and (12) Texas and United States history as individual subjects and in reading courses.

Marvin Veselka is Associate Commissioner for Professional Support, Texas Education Agency.

As in many other states, the "back-to-basics" movement was prevalent in Texas. In fact, the legislature directed the repeal of all existing statutory requirements for curriculum and authorized the State Board of Education to establish a new curriculum for the public schools. The board was to define the content of the 12 subject areas by grade level and course.

Thus, in 1981, Texas educators faced two new legislative mandates: initiate teacher certification testing and develop a new state-mandated curriculum. The certification testing law contained a protection clause for students who were already enrolled in teacher certification programs in that the State Board of Education called for the first certification test to take place in the spring of 1986. This 1986 date placed the incoming freshman class in the fall of 1982 on notice that, upon graduation, a requirement for certification would include successful performance on both subject-matter and pedagogy tests.

Essential Elements

Immediately following the close of the 1981 legislative session, work began on the development of the state-mandated curriculum. A vast number of educators took part in developing and refining the content of the Essential Elements of the Curriculum. It was understood that the Essential Elements would describe the curriculum to be taught. Each school district would be required to provide instruction in the Essential Elements at the appropriate grade level. School districts were given license to add elements, but they could not delete or omit content as required by the State Board of Education.

The Essential Elements are broad objectives representing the core knowledge, skills, and competencies that all students should learn to be effective and productive members of society. Texas developed Essential Elements for every subject taught in the elementary grades PK-6, and for every secondary course offered in grades 7-12. This undertaking, culminating in a single state-mandated curriculum to be taught in all 1,069 school districts in Texas, was the first of its kind in the nation. The breadth and scope of the effort are impressive.

Certification Testing

Work on the curriculum reforms was completed in 1983. However, the Texas Education Agency (TEA) did not call for bids on teacher certification test development until the summer of 1984. By that time, the state had decided that a program of criterion-referenced tests specifically developed for use in Texas would be the most effective means of assessing future teachers' competencies. A number of factors led to this decision, including the desire to customize the tests to our unique curriculum and to assure all persons an equal opportunity to prepare for these tests.

The demographic composition of Texas is changing rapidly. More than 30 percent of our student population and more than 10 percent of our teachers are Hispanic. We are rapidly approaching the time when the Hispanic and black populations combined will be a majority in our system. We felt that a custom testing program would best address equity concerns for minority candidates by ensuring that the tests assess the specific knowledge requisite for performance in Texas classrooms.

DEVELOPMENT PROCESS

The process used in test development was seen as an important aspect of the validity issue. The steps in the process included delineating job-domain objectives, conducting a job analysis, specifying how objectives were to be operationalized, writing items, field testing, and validating test content. The Texas series of steps was not unique, yet all procedures were customized for Texas.

The design of the testing program calls for 64 tests to be developed based upon certificates issued by the state of Texas: 34 tests in Phase I and 30 tests in Phase II. The key to the design was the job analysis in each testing field. We wanted to ensure that the content measured on each test was job related and consistent with Texas public school practice. Using the Essential Elements as a basis for test content was not enough to ensure job relatedness. An effort was also made to document the amount of usage and the importance of the objectives in the classroom.

The design called for the selection of a ten-member advisory committee for each test area. By a State Board of Education directive, six members of each committee were public school educators and four were college or university faculty. Of the four faculty members, at least two were from the discipline of the test area. For example, the committee for secondary mathematics included two college or university faculty members from a school of arts and sciences mathematics department. The purpose of this stipulation was to reflect academic rigor.

COMMITTEE SELECTION

Selecting advisory committees was a major task. We were fortunate to have had a high degree of interest in the program among educators. Nomination forms were sent to all 1,069 school districts, 66 colleges and universities, and all of the professional education associations in the state. The forms asked for detailed information, including teaching assignment, area of expertise, ethnicity, and associational or institutional affiliation. This extensive search enabled us to make committee selections that collectively represented all parts and population groups of the state. Nominations exceeded 4,500 and, as of today, approximately 1,050 Texas educators have served on our committees.

The committees were vital to the development process. The test development contractor and TEA staff had established a draft content framework for each test area which consisted of major subareas, clusters of objectives, and content limits that specified individual objectives. Each committee reviewed and revised the framework and objectives in its field, at times making numerous revisions. Committee decisions were final.

The contractor, National Evaluation Systems, Inc., used the revisions to develop item specifications as a guide to item writing. These specifications, along with the content limits, made explicit the content to be measured for each objective, as approved by the committees.

After the job analysis surveys were completed, committees reviewed the results and made the final selections of job-related objectives to be measured on the test. Advisory committees were also instrumental in reviewing and revising draft test items prior to field tryouts. In all, each committee met four times. Thus, every item used in the Texas program is the result of committee review at several stages of development.

BIAS REVIEW

Special advisory committees also participated in the development process. Their purpose was to review and suggest revision of test items to avoid potential bias of any sort (e.g., ethnic, racial). These panels, one in each test field, were composed solely of minority group members.

STANDARD SETTING

Additional advisory committees, similarly composed but of different individuals, were used in an independent validation and standard-setting procedure for the tests in each field. These committees reviewed each test question against its objective, considered other evaluative criteria (e.g., potential bias), and participated in making recommendations of passing scores. While the details of these procedures are beyond the scope of this chapter, it is important to note that this last review involved individuals with no prior involvement in the test development process. Their independence is a critical aspect of the validation procedures for the instruments.

TEST VALIDITY

The validity of the tests in the Examination for the Certification of Educators in Texas (ExCET) program is endemic to the development process. Texas did not take existing tests and validate them. Rather, the TEA elected to create tests using a process that built validity into the tests at every stage. The repeated involvement of the several advisory committees in each testing field, the job analysis surveys with thousands of Texas classroom teachers and teacher educators, the extensive field test, and the independent validation of items create a direct link between test content and actual classroom teaching practices. That link is the key to validity in testing programs such as ExCET.

Other Program Components

There are other important aspects of the project that contribute to its character. Early in the project, the TEA published a brochure that provided background information on the ExCET and answered a series of commonly asked questions about the program. Brochures were provided to the 66 colleges and universities that train teachers in Texas with directions to distribute them to all students in teacher education programs.

The colleges and universities also received guides of annotated test objectives. The sets of objectives, organized by content area, included all those objectives eligible for inclusion on the tests.

STUDY GUIDES

Another valuable feature of the program is the distribution of specific study guides for all testing areas. These guides contain information about the testing program, helpful hints on study and preparation, a list of the annotated objectives that are eligible to be measured, and a practice test. The practice test items are products of the same development process described earlier; the practice test is, therefore, an excellent indicator of the difficulty of the actual examination. The answer keys for the practice test include explanations of the correct answers.

The net effect of these features is to assure that examinees and the institutions that prepare them are aware of test content. Examinees have the information necessary to prepare for the tests or for remediation.

The Examination for the Certification of Educators in Texas is, in our estimation, the most valid testing program that could be offered as a prerequisite for licensure of educators. The goal was clear: develop tests that measure the content knowledge expected of entry-level teachers and administrators in Texas schools. We have achieved that outcome because we defined specifically what each test should measure in terms of curriculum, and we implemented a process that made that definition a reality. Moreover, we created a program with many custom features that accommodate the state's needs.

Educational reform is just beginning, and the new teachers being granted Texas certificates will play a major role in the changes to occur in the next decade. Tests like those in the ExCET program will play a pivotal part in changing teacher education to prepare individuals for teaching.

Excellence and Equity in Teacher Competency Testing: A Policy Perspective

Bernard R. Gifford

The Teacher Testing Movement

Since the National Commission on Excellence in Education issued *A Nation at Risk: The Imperative for Educational Reform* in 1983, a plethora of teacher assessment laws and regulations has been enacted by the states. As of 1985, 31 states have adopted some form of testing policy for prospective teachers (U.S. Department of Education, 1986). In most cases, as a result of their own initiative or at the insistence of governors and legislatures, state departments of education have instituted a standardized examination, established a cutoff score, and prohibited teacher candidates from proceeding any further in their pursuit of a teaching career until they have passed the test. In a few instances, state education departments have mandated that licensed, working teachers pass an examination to retain their certification, and at least one state educational agency has linked merit pay increases to teacher testing.

VARIED REQUIREMENTS

State policies vary as to when prospective teachers must take examinations, whether basic skills and/or general, professional, or subject-matter knowledge are tested, and what the minimum passing score is for a given test. Twenty-one states currently require students to pass an examination for admission into a teacher preparation program, and 31 require teacher candidates to pass a test for certification; the numbers overlap (Anrig, 1986). Either singly or in combination, several tests are used for admission, including the Scholastic Aptitude Test (SAT), the American College Testing program (ACT), the California Achievement Test, the Pre-Professional Skills Test (P-PST), the National Teacher Examination (NTE) Core Battery, and state-developed examinations. In the case of the SAT, minimum passing scores range from combined scores of 745 to 1,000. For certification, most states use the NTE Core Battery, the NTE Specialty Area tests, and/or their own state-

---

Bernard R. Gifford is Dean of the Graduate School of Education at the University of California at Berkeley.

developed examinations. Passing scores vary. For example, the grading scale of the NTE Specialty Area Test in Elementary School Education is 250 to 990, and the cutoff scores range from 480 to 600 points (Goertz & Pitcher, 1985, p. 3).

In California, for instance, prospective teachers who have not completed a study program designed to insure subject area expertise are required to score above a specific minimum cutoff score on an appropriate NTE subject area test. Since 1983, they must also take the California Basic Educational Skills Test (CBEST), which is designed to measure basic skills in mathematics, reading, and writing. They must take the test for diagnostic purposes before they are permitted to student teach and must pass it prior to certification.

Professional Response

With varying degrees of enthusiasm, the concept of teacher testing has been accepted by members of the profession. Until recently, the National Education Association (NEA) vigorously opposed the use of tests as a criterion for teacher certification, evaluation, or promotion. It has argued that standardized examinations are: 1) "biased against those who are economically disadvantaged or who are culturally and linguistically different"; 2) "invalid, unreliable, out of date and restricted to the measurement of cognitive skills"; 3) "used by book publishers and testing companies to promote their financial interests rather than improve measurement and instruction"; and 4) "used by the media as a basis for invidious comparisons" (National Education Association, 1980, p. 51). However, at its July 1985 national convention, the NEA partially reversed its longstanding position and adopted a stance in favor of requiring prospective teachers to pass valid and unbiased pedagogical and subject-matter tests.

In contrast, the American Federation of Teachers (AFT) has for some time actively supported the use of "accurate and appropriate measures to certify teachers" (Scherer, 1983, p. 49). Indeed, in 1985, Albert Shanker, the president of the AFT, proposed the development of a national teacher examination comparable in rigor to those used in the legal and medical professions. He announced that the AFT is prepared to limit its membership to those who have passed such a test (Shanker, 1985).

Teachers at the grass-roots level also appear to be receptive to testing. According to the 1984 Gallup Poll of Teachers' Attitudes

Toward the Public Schools, 63 percent of the respondents expressed support for "a state board examination to prove their knowledge in the subjects they plan to teach" (Gallup, 1984, p. 107). However, a defensive reaction to public fears of teacher incompetence, rather than confidence in testing and their own professionalism, may have engendered this view among teachers.

TEACHER TESTING POLICY IMPACTS

While the concept of teacher testing seems to have gained at least the verbal endorsement of teachers and their representatives, the implementation of specific teacher testing policies remains highly problematic. For example, while state superintendents have generally advocated the use of teacher examinations, they are concerned that cutoff scores do not reflect standards of excellence. Instead, passing scores may simply represent minimal levels of proficiency that are politically acceptable and that do not threaten to reduce the supply of teachers. Evidence of a trend in this direction has been identified by the ad hoc Committee on Competency Tests and Performance Assessment of the Council of Chief State School Officers (Scherer, 1983, pp. 59-60).

In addition, while many deans of schools of education support teacher candidate testing as a means of improving the overall quality of their students, they pay a price for this quality increase: an immediate enrollment decline. Some have argued that the short-term fall in enrollment will be more than offset by a long-term increase in the enrollment of higher-quality prospective teachers. As evidence of the benefits of this "addition by subtraction" policy, the example of the University of Oregon has been cited. Following its decision to raise admission standards, the university experienced, for the first time in its history, a waiting list to enroll in its teacher education program (Pugach & Raths, 1983). What is not clear is whether Oregon actually increased the relative attractiveness of teacher training vis-a-vis other programs of study for academically accomplished students or merely denied entry to students who would have been admitted under former standards. Unless teaching attracts a greater proportion of academically able students, the "addition by subtraction" argument remains unconfirmed and troublesome. For a dean of a school of education in an institution experiencing an overall enrollment decline, raising admissions standards may be risky in the face of counterpressure to relax eligibility criteria in order to boost the number of students.

At the same time, some deans of schools of education are confronted with the prospect of state policies linking teacher candidate testing to accreditation. As a result of a 1984 law, teacher preparation programs in Tennessee are placed on probation for one year if 30 percent or more of their students fail the state's basic skills test. If a 30 percent or more failure rate persists for two consecutive years, a teacher training program's accreditation is revoked. In Florida, a similar law resulted in 18 out of the state's 25 teacher training institutions losing state approval of one or more of their educational programs (Stoddart, Losk, & Benson, 1984, p. 7). This punitive approach misplaces accountability for educational malpractice. Developing the basic skills of prospective teachers is not a focus of teacher preparation programs, but of K-12 and undergraduate education as a whole.

OTHER PROFESSIONAL PROGRAMS

Furthermore, other professional schools are not subject to similar fates when large proportions of their students fail licensure examinations. For example, in California, the failure rate for the February sitting of the state bar examination is usually around 72 percent. While the state bar does rank California law schools according to their student passing rates for some purposes, no one has suggested that a law school should have its accreditation revoked because of the relatively poor showing of some of its students on the bar examination.

Law students are seen as individually responsible for acquiring a considerable body of skills and knowledge prior to entry into a true profession characterized by autonomous decision making. In contrast, the common perception is that teacher candidates are products molded by their schools, given a veneer of competency, and sent into a semiprofession highly constrained by governors, legislatures, state and local commissions and boards, superintendents, and principals. Consequently, while lawyers and law schools are accorded high status, teachers and schools of education are not.

Correspondingly, while the public assumes that law schools can be trusted to operate in accordance with free market principles—competing with one another for the best students with state bar pass rates as the indicator of success—it views teacher training institutions with suspicion. Teacher training institutions, it is presumed, are likely to recruit—off the street, as it were—just about anyone, with little regard for the impact on their own effectiveness as educational enterprises or on the quality of the nation's teaching force. Although this exaggeration is rarely true, it has been true enough, often enough, for many policy makers, both outside and inside the educational establishment, to lose confidence in teacher training institutions.

For more than 125 years, states have used tests to screen unqualified persons from teaching. In fact, teacher testing was predominant until the 1920s and 1930s, when educational reformers urged that tests be abandoned in favor of rigorous teacher preparation by first-rate teaching schools and colleges (Vold, 1985). With the revival of teacher testing as a critical issue in contemporary educational reform, it is therefore incumbent upon schools and colleges of education to boldly strengthen and improve their programs. Revitalization and innovation are necessary if teacher training institutions are to insure their own viability and if teaching professionals are to meet standards of excellence. The status and prospects of teacher education and the teaching profession are inextricably connected (Gifford, 1984a, 1984b, 1985).

The Impact of Testing on Minorities

With greater reliance on both student and teacher testing, the longstanding controversy surrounding use of standardized examinations has intensified. Among those most reluctant to sanction widespread use of standardized tests are individuals and groups concerned about the disparate impact of the examinations on prospective teachers from minority backgrounds.

PASSING RATES

According to the Commission on Teacher Credentialing (1984), of 6,644 minority candidates who took the first CBEST in 1983, 3,854, or 58 percent, failed. The highest failure rate was among blacks. Of the 2,040 blacks who took the exam, only 530, or a paltry 26 percent, were able to proceed with their plans to be teachers. For other minority groups, the test results were not much better. Only 834 out of 2,133, or 39 percent, of Mexican Americans and only 50 percent, or 637 out of 1, 259, Asian Americans passed the CBEST exam. In comparison, the passing rate for whites was 76 percent, with 18,856 of the 24,540 whites passing.

The passing rates elsewhere are no more encouraging. Of a total of 5,500 teachers certified in Florida in 1981, only 200 were black. This low number was mirrored in the passing rates on Florida's

Teacher Competency Examination, given for the first time in 1983. While 90 percent of white candidates passed the examination, only 35 percent of black candidates, 51 percent of Hispanic candidates, and 63 percent of Asian candidates passed (Smith, 1984, p. 7).

The first administration of the Texas testing program for entry to teacher education programs, using the P-PST, eliminated 84 percent of the black candidates and 65 percent of the Hispanic candidates on the basis of the mathematics examination. Eighty-seven percent of the black candidates and 65 percent of the Hispanic candidates failed the reading test, and 80 percent of the black candidates and 56 percent of the Hispanic candidates failed the writing test (Smith, 1984, p. 8).

The problems associated with these high minority failure rates are made all the more serious by the increasing need for qualified black, Hispanic, and Asian American teachers at a time of rapid demographic change. California data illustrate the national trend. In the 1984-85 school year, the state's total public school population was 53.1 percent non-Hispanic white; 27.9 percent were Hispanic, 9.7 percent were black, 8.5 percent were Asian or Pacific Islanders, and 0.8 percent were American Indian. It is projected that more than 50 percent of the state's total public school population will be nonwhite by 1995. If California's public schools indeed become more than 50 percent nonwhite, they will join the schools in the nation's 35 largest city school districts, the majority of which now have overwhelmingly minority student enrollments. Needless to say, the combination of high minority failure rates on teacher examinations and high minority pupil enrollment rates, if unchecked by dramatic interventions, could result in a high degree of tension between minority parents and a largely nonminority teaching staff. A conflict between communities and schools similar to that which plagued public education during the 1960s in many of the nation's major urban areas could ensue.

Two Trends

INTEREST IN TEACHING

The rates of failure on teacher examinations reflect two ominous trends. First, interest in teaching on the part of many well-educated students, especially talented minority students, has declined precipitously in the last 15 years. As the teacher surplus of the 1970s drastically reduced job opportunities, college students increasingly chose other majors. Moreover, as new career opportunities outside education have opened up for them, the best and brightest minority and women students, who earlier might have entered teaching, have chosen other fields. The proportion of college-bound students who indicated they intended to major in education fell from 24 percent in 1969 to less than 5 percent in 1982. The decline has been particularly evident among highly qualified minorities and women.

COLLEGE PROGRAMS

Second, colleges and universities are failing to guarantee that their graduates, both minority and nonminority, can read with comprehension, write literately, and perform routine mathematical computations. This trend is but an overt manifestation of the general failure of many colleges and universities to exercise proper leadership and authority over their educational programs. The American Association of Colleges, in its report "Integrity in the College Curriculum: A Report to the Academic Community" (1985), maintains that decline and devaluation are evident everywhere. Moreover,

> there is so much confusion as to the mission of the American college and university that it is no longer possible to be sure why a student should take a particular program of courses. Is the curriculum an invitation to philosophic and intellectual growth or a quick exposure to the skills of a particular vocation? Or is it both? Certainty on such matters disappeared under the impact of new knowledge and electives in the late nineteenth century. The subsequent collapse of structure and control in the course of study has invited the intrusion of programs of ephemeral knowledge developed without concern for the criteria of self-discovery, critical thinking, and exploration of values that were for so long central to the baccalaureate years. The curriculum has given way to a marketplace philosophy: it is a supermarket where students are shoppers and professors are merchants of learning. Fads and fashions, the demands of popularity and success, enter where wisdom and experience should prevail. Does it make sense for a college to offer a thousand courses to a student who will only take 36?
>
> The marketplace philosophy refuses to establish common expectations and norms. Another victim of this posture of irresponsibility is the general education of the American college undergraduate, the institutional course requirements outside the major. They lack a rationale and cohesion or, even worse, are almost lacking altogether. Electives are being used to fatten majors and diminish breadth. It is as if no one cared, so long as the store stays open. (p. 12)

If this trend persists—and make no mistake about it, it will, as long as colleges and universities, ignoring the implications of the findings contained in "Integrity in the College Curriculum," continue to permit unknowledgeable students to chart their own intellectual development—the situation will only deteriorate further. Unaided by the collective intelligence of the academic community and lacking a commitment by higher education institutions to the improvement of the attractiveness of the teaching profession, the supply of talented, well-educated minority teachers will continue to nosedive.

DECLINING MINORITY TEACHER CANDIDATES

In Florida, where applicants for teacher training programs must score a minimum of 835 on the SAT, Professor Walter A. Mercer (1983) of Florida Agricultural and Mechanical University, a historically black college supported by the state, predicts that "future teachers from [minority] groups could become vanishing breeds" (p. 29). In Texas, where candidates for certification must pass reading, writing, and mathematics tests, researchers estimate that by 1988, 96 percent of black candidates and 84 percent of Hispanic candidates will be denied permission to teach on the basis of their reading tests alone. They also project that minority representation in the national teaching force could be reduced to less than 5 percent by 1990, if the currently observable trend in passing rates continues unabated and if rates of attrition through retirements and teacher burnout are unchanged (Smith, 1984, p. 7).

These figures are both disturbing and unacceptable. They have a devastating effect on young adults who have a strong desire to build careers for themselves by educating our children. Their impact is also to deny minority groups access to exemplars of success. Moreover, there is the awful possibility that minority youth, upon learning that many prospective minority teachers are judged not good enough to teach, will lose confidence in their own abilities and conclude that higher education is off limits to them.

The first reaction of many to the apparent negative relationship between testing and the potential supply of minority teachers is to claim "racism" and to insist that alternate certification standards be adopted for minority candidates. Certainly, if the implication of this connection is ignored, there is the real possibility that the promise of democracy and the promise of equality will be placed, yet again, in deep jeopardy. The question remains whether this prospect necessarily rules out the use of proficiency tests.

In Favor of Competency Testing of Minority Candidates

AN ANALOGY

Many insights into the need for proficiency testing are gained by analyzing the analogous arguments advanced by sociologist Harry Edwards (1983) of the University of California at Berkeley, regarding Rule 48 of the National Collegiate Athletic Association (NCAA). The passage of this rule sparked "what is probably the most heated race-related controversy within the NCAA since the onset of widespread racial integration in major college sports programs during the 1950s and 1960s" (p. 33). Effective in 1986, the rule requires freshmen who want to participate in sports at any of the nation's 277 Division I colleges and universities to have attained a minimum combined score of 700 or a composite score of 15 on the ACT. In addition, they must have achieved a C average in 11 specific high school courses, including English, mathematics, social sciences, and physical sciences.

The response of many black educators to Rule 48 was sharp and immediate. Some were angered because they were not consulted in the formulation of the new policy; others claimed that the SAT minimum score was set arbitrarily. Still others stated that the SAT and the ACT are racist diagnostic tests, biased in favor of white students, and that the proposed cutoffs impose unfair penalties on black athletes.

In contrast, Edwards (1983) took a stand supporting the enforcement of Rule 48. He agreed that the determination of the cutoff scores may well have been arbitrary, but found them so arbitrarily low as to constitute no standard at all. Edwards stated:

> Further, were I not to support Rule 48, I would risk communicating to black youth in particular that I, a nationally known black educator, do not believe that they have the capacity to achieve a 700 score on the SAT, with three years to prepare for the test, when they are given a total of 400 points simply for answering a single question in each of the two sections of the test, and when they have a significant chance of scoring 460 by a purely random marking of the test. Finally, I support the NCAA's action because I believe that black parents, black educators and the black community must insist that black children be taught and that they learn whatever subject matter is necessary to excel on diagnostic and all other skills tests. (p. 37)

The argument of Edwards is both compelling and persuasive. However, it is also incomplete. It is clear that if Edwards's view

is to be translated into policy, support of minimum competency
rules must be coupled with insistence that minority children receive
a sufficiently high-quality education to enable them to score
competitively on examinations from SAT, to CBEST, to NTE. It is
also clear that state public officials, in and out of the education
establishment, must commit themselves to develop, fund,
vigorously monitor, and intelligently evaluate targeted school
improvement programs so that minority students at all levels can
become more competitive on all examinations of scholastic
achievement.

Current Tests

VALIDITY

This position does not assume that standardized examinations
are problem free or totally unbiased. Clearly, there is no evidence
that the teacher tests currently being used have predictive validity
(Cronin, 1983). They do not discriminate between those who will
become effective or ineffective teachers. Some individuals who pass
the tests will indeed become incompetent teachers. This caveat
must be brought to the forefront of policy discussions concerning
teacher testing.

There is also evidence that some current tests are lacking in
content validity. The present NTE Core Battery, for example, was
designed by the Educational Testing Service (ETS) with the
assistance of panels of teacher educators and teaching practitioners
who were asked to judge the face validity of the test items (Anrig,
1986, pp. 447-451). While ETS adhered to strict standards of test
quality and fairness and asked independent groups, including the
NEA and the AFT, to select multiracial panel members, there are
two main problems with this approach.

First, the Core Battery is purported to represent a consensus
among educators as to the knowledge important to an entry-level
teacher (Educational Testing Service, 1983b, p. 19). However, in
fact, there is little agreement among practitioners and researchers
as to what beginning teachers need to know. The judgments of
ETS panelists about test item validity may therefore have been
situational, subjective, and idiosyncratic. In implicit recognition of
this probability, ETS requires each state that chooses to administer
the NTE to conduct its own content validity study. However, this
policy does not increase confidence in the NTE's validity. Using the
same basic methodology described above, ETS itself has conducted

60 percent (21) of the state studies (Cross, 1985, pp. 7-9). While as many as 38 percent of the test items have been identified as invalid for a given state (National Evaluation Systems, Inc., 1985, p. 4), the NTE has not been modified accordingly but continues to be administered as originally designed.

Second, the content of the Core Battery appears to be more closely related to the curricula of teacher preparation programs than to the competency of effective beginning teachers. According to ETS, the tests "were developed to provide information about a candidate's knowledge and skills, typically acquired through a teacher-training program" (Educational Testing Service, 1983a, p. 7). Especially in light of the manifest need to reform teacher education programs, it cannot be assumed that the objectives and content of teacher training curricula reflect the proficiency areas or levels possessed by capable entry-level teachers. That this concern has substance is supported by ETS's recent undertaking of a job analysis study involving 16,000 practicing teachers (Anrig, 1986, pp. 447-451). Presumably, the results will be used to increase the job relatedness of the NTE.

David Owen, in his 1985 critique of the ETS, suggests that the NTE's present lack of relevance to the workplace constitutes grounds for the abandonment of the examination. Since the Pre-Professional Skills Test seems to be an abbreviated version of the NTE, he advises states to avoid this examination as well. Owen further asserts that the quality of the teaching profession is in fact reduced by the NTE in that its relationship to teacher training curricula reinforces the mediocrity of such programs. He states that the "easiest way to improve on the NTE would be to get rid of it" (p. 258).

However, this is a simplistic and unrealistic response to a complicated issue. Tests that do have content validity and are properly used can perform a useful function in assessing teacher competency. The development of better tests, then, is the appropriate public policy priority.

POTENTIAL BIAS

In addition to validity issues, some teacher tests have been questioned on the basis of potential bias in favor of or against particular racial, socioeconomic, and other groups. Bias can be difficult to substantiate, and the elimination of test bias can be equally problematic.

In 1981, for example, a class action suit was filed against the Alabama State Board of Education on the grounds that the state's teacher competency testing program discriminated against blacks and violated their constitutional and statutory civil rights (*Allen v. Alabama State Board of Education*, 1986). One provision of the multifaceted consent decree in favor of the plaintiffs required the state to delete test questions that showed black/white performance differentials of more than 15 percent (Rebell, 1986).[1] If implemented, this remedy might have resulted in the deletion of a large number of test items, an action that would have removed race bias while simultaneously distorting the job relatedness of the testing program. Since the job relatedness of the test appears to have been carefully established—the test developer, National Evaluation Systems, Inc., consulted more than 5,000 Alabama teachers—the net gain to the plaintiffs on the issue of test revision might have been minimal. This dilemma may have been a factor in the presiding judge's decision to vacate the consent decree in February 1986.

The case for the class bias of some of the currently used tests is less clouded. Allan Nairn (1980) says of the SAT, "In sum, it is advertised as a test of scholastic aptitude . . . used by colleges to accept and reject applicants ostensibly on the basis of merit. For many students, the SAT may be more a reflection of their social class than of their potential for accomplishment inside or beyond the classroom" (p. 652). Mary Frances Berry furthers this argument with her assertion that the major differential among SAT test scores is "not between black and white students, but between students from well-off families and students from poor families. The better-off the family, the higher the score—for whites *and* blacks" (Edwards, 1983, p. 34). Indeed, the College Board's 1984 report *Profiles of College-Bound Seniors* shows exactly that. The relationship between family income and SAT test scores is highly significant. While not as high, the relationship between level of parental education and SAT scores of high school seniors is also very substantial.

On the question of test fairness, Banesh Hoffman (1962) goes even further in maintaining that the SAT is biased against everyone with a penetrating mind. Of the SAT's multiple-choice format, he observes:

> How genuinely difficult, how worthy of first-rate minds, can questions be for which answers must be picked at the rate of one every minute or so, or in some cases, at the rate of a hundred an hour? How deeply can such questions probe and still be machine-gradable? And if the questions did indeed have depth, how could one reasonably expect the candidates to give well-considered

responses to them so quickly? Is it likely that students who can maintain a lively interest in long successions of small, efficient conundrums are those with deep minds, or even those with an adult set of values? (p. 89)

From Analysis to Policy

Clearly, there must be vigilance in insuring the proper use of standardized tests in assessing the competency of potential teachers. The testing industry must be persuaded to revise and design tests that are both unbiased and valid. Where necessary, legal action should be strongly considered as an avenue for testing reform and policy change. There must also be full understanding about what standardized tests can and cannot do. To quote *Washington Post* columnist William Raspberry, standardized tests cannot:

> measure patience, love of children and learning, the ability to maintain order and a hundred other things that make up teacher competency. But the tests can measure whether a teacher has learned the basics of pedagogic techniques (which we consider important, else why would we mandate education courses for teachers?) and whether a teacher has a solid grasp of the material to be taught . . . (Brott, 1983, p. 37).

This view is strongly endorsed. While tests cannot be relied upon to identify who has the personal warmth, caring, drive, and dedication required of a good teacher, they can provide some reliable information about the basic competencies of a pool of applicants. Further, good standardized tests, more than measuring potential aptitude, indicate what students have learned; they also show how well students are able to apply their learning to what the test asks of them.

DEALING WITH MINORITY FAILURE

The question remains, however, how do we break the cycle of minority failure on teacher tests? Again, William Raspberry has insight into the crux of the problem: ". . .the reason minority applicants fare worse on the tests than whites is that they themselves are victims of inferior schooling" (Brott, 1983, p. 37). Therefore, what teacher test results indicate is that the education of our children, especially those from minority and low-income families, must be improved. Rejecting what Arnold M. Gallegos (1984), Dean of the College of Education at Northern Arizona

University, correctly describes as our historical tendency to "blame the victims" for their failure on examinations, we must instead focus on the reform of the educational institutions that prepare our students.

EDUCATIONAL REFORM

A priority in this effort is to increase the financial allocations made to colleges and schools of education. An underlying cause of the low minority passing rates on teacher competency tests is inequities in the resources devoted to teacher training institutions, particularly historically black colleges. Ipso facto, resource-poor teacher colleges and schools of education, no matter how high the innate ability of their students, are disadvantaged in providing the breadth, intensity, and level of education needed by future teachers. If higher education institutions are strengthened, then the skills and knowledge of future teachers will be advanced.

In California, the most recent passing rates on the CBEST augur well for the potential benefits of maintaining minimum teacher competency standards while focusing on educational reform. In 1985, 33 percent of black examinees passed the test, a figure 7 percent higher than the 1983 number cited earlier. Among Mexican Americans, the passing rate was 46 percent, also a 7 percent improvement. Representing a 6 percent increase, 56 percent of Asian Americans met minimum competency standards. Among whites, 81 percent passed, 5 percent more than in 1983 (Watkins, 1985, p. 14). These figures suggest that higher education institutions and teacher candidates have recognized the implications of past CBEST scores, conducted self-evaluations, and made decisions that have led to higher-quality programs and higher-quality students.

If note is taken of Henry Levin's provocative finding that each additional point scored by teachers on their SAT verbal subtest can be translated into a net gain of .175 points on the verbal scores of black students and .179 on the verbal scores of white students (Weaver, 1984, p. 110), then there is even more impetus to provide educational settings that will give all students the same chance at passing teacher credentialing examinations, regardless of their racial or socioeconomic backgrounds.

Direct action must be taken to provide all students in our public schools with quality education that is responsive to their real needs. This effort depends on the existence of well-qualified teachers, including well-qualified minority teachers. To meet this challenge while also maintaining and improving standards of excellence, the pool of qualified minority teachers must be enlarged.

All of the knowledge and skills that are tested in competency examinations are learnable. Students can achieve acceptable test scores if they are taught what they need to know. This means teaching all of the skills and understanding that they will require to function well in the contemporary world and to be prepared to make the best adaptations and choices in their lives as they move into the future.

A Proposal

Toward this end, a comprehensive proposal is offered. While it will bring a transitional period of short-run disappointment for some who will be locked out of the teacher training programs they wish to enter, the plan will finally put a stop to "victim blaming" measures that have created more problems each time they have been applied in place of long-ranged, well-articulated solutions. The proposal consists of three steps: the early recruitment and intensive training of minority and low-income students who have a commitment to teaching; the implementation of improved teacher selection policies; and the identification and reward of outstanding teachers.

Step One: The Early Recruitment and Intensive Training of Minority and Low-Income Students Who Wish to Teach

As early as high school, students who have expressed interest in teaching as a career would be selected to participate in a special university preprofessional teacher preparation program. The program would consist of a five-year course of study leading to the bachelor's degree and would provide a series of paid school year and summer teaching-related internships. In addition to the traditional criteria of grades and past achievements, program admission standards would consider potential for growth and an exceptionally strong willingness to learn. Special efforts would be made to attract students with a background or interest in areas of special need, such as mathematics and science or language and literacy.

BASIC SKILLS DIAGNOSIS

Upon entry into the program, optimally with entry into college, students would be given a series of criterion-referenced tests for diagnostic purposes. In conjunction with their regular course load, the students would be enrolled in a series of self-paced tutorials to work on basic skills development in those areas where their diagnostic tests indicate attention is needed. These tutorials would be an integral part of a substantive undergraduate liberal arts program. They would be designed to do away with troublesome conditions such as those identified in Stanley Ivie's analysis of black student achievement on the NTE.

Ivie (1982) notes that black students perform poorly on the NTE because the examination is as much a reading test as a subject-matter test. Consequently, many black students cannot perform well on the test because of inadequate reading skills. Ivie observes that most black students have not "mastered the basics" prior to entering college; moreover, colleges do little to correct the situation because of an insufficient emphasis on the teaching of writing and because of policies that allow students to avoid liberal arts courses that have substance or rigor. Given such circumstances, it is sadly understandable why tests taken at the end of college too often show poor results.

In response to these needs, the proposed developmental program would focus at the undergraduate level on reading skills; basic mathematics operations, with heavy emphasis on reasoning skills, manipulations, and application; and good, clear writing. Since the students would at the same time be enrolled in subject-matter courses that require these skills, they would have sufficient opportunities to practice the skills as they were developing and to receive continual feedback as they utilized new skills in their course work. At the end of two years, the students would take a series of tests to measure their growth. A new set of self-paced tutorials, based upon their current skill levels, would be developed, and the process would be repeated on a higher level. The students would also take practice versions of the required teacher licensing examinations.

The licensing tests themselves should not be used as diagnostic tools unless improved. There have been problems, for example, in using the CBEST for this purpose. Richard Watkins, CBEST consultant to the California Commission on Teacher Credentialing, notes that far greater demands are made on a test to be used for diagnosis than for determining proficiency, since a diagnostic test must "yield reliable measurement over a continuum of skill or ability and provide reliable scores on several reasonably different skills and subskills" (California Postsecondary Education Commission, 1984, p. 7). Watkins cautions that tests such as the CBEST can only make the most general predictions about outcomes and cannot be used for prescription on the basis of their results alone. This explains the lack of success for those who have failed the CBEST and attempted to use their test results as a basis of preparation for reexamination. The candidates who have done this have been frustrated and angered by their lack of progress. The approach recommended above would avoid this situation by providing accurate diagnostic tools (e.g., genuine criterion-referenced tests) combined with practice on the actual test to gain familiarity with and confidence in standardized test taking.

GRADUATE STUDY

Upon satisfactory completion of the undergraduate program and the conferral of the bachelor's degree, students would be guaranteed admission to participating colleges and universities (e.g., the California State University teacher education programs or the University of California Graduate Schools of Education). Graduate scholarships covering the full costs of student fees and filing expenses would be provided to all entering students with an undergraduate grade point average of B+ or better. Partial tuition scholarships would be available to those with a B average. The students would, of course, also have access to regular financial aid programs. Again, as in the first phase of this program, paid internships would be provided to all qualified students for the duration of their graduate teacher training studies.

NEEDED CHANGES

Given present realities, several things will have to be changed before we can proceed seriously with this program—and only one of them involves raising the competency level of future teachers. To attract and retain the best and brightest applicants, society must accord them the same status given to young professionals in other career fields. Only then will the public have the right to expect high-level professional performance and long-range staying power from them. In terms of the minority and low-income candidates who must be recruited, the polity will have to affirm its national commitment to quality education and underwrite, through federal and state contributions, the creation of excellence. This would require incentives to potential teachers in the form of scholarships and loans with forgiveness provisions based upon number of years of service as a teacher. To attract good people, it is also necessary to make serious efforts to bring teaching salaries into the professional range. In California, this process has just begun. Many hope that it is not too little too late.

Step Two: The Selection of Highly Qualified Teaching Professionals

Despite the current situation—that of being at the end of a period of oversupply of teachers—teacher personnel policies would be redesigned based upon the recommendations made in the report *Race, Ethnicity and Equal Employment Opportunity: An Investigation of Access to Employment and Assignment of Professional Personnel in New York City's Public Schools* (Gifford, 1977).

TERMINATE "ALTERNATIVE" SELECTION

First, any existing "alternative" teacher selection policies would be terminated. Although such programs may have been successful in increasing minority employment opportunities, they have operated as racial conduits, steering newly hired minority teachers into almost exclusively minority schools. Given minority applicants who have undergone rigorous training, the rationale for alternative selection policies would disappear. There would be significant advances toward reversing the persistent pattern in which teachers with fewer years of experience, less advanced training, and lower salaries are assigned to schools with high proportions of minority and low-income pupils. As soon as these teachers gain enough seniority to do so, they move on to "better" schools populated with middle- and high-income students. This phenomenon would be offset by the development of systems of equal employment opportunity goals and plans that integrate school faculties and show all school children that both quality education and the achievement of high test scores are functions of many factors, but that group membership is no longer one of them.

Second, traditional systems for the selection and evaluation of new teachers would be replaced with ones that encourage personnel officials to match the needs of students in the public schools more closely with the talents of potential teachers in the applicant pool. The effectiveness of our school systems will not be found in the statistics on the racial composition of our teaching staffs, but rather in the statistics reflecting our students' mastery of basic skills in reading, writing, and arithmetic. Nevertheless, it must be understood that proportional minority participation in the teaching career and high-quality outcomes in terms of student learning are not at odds with each other. There is no such thing as a choice between equity and excellence. There is no equity in the absence of excellence.

Step Three: Identifying and Rewarding Outstanding Teachers

In addition to existing teacher tests, a new one would be designed and implemented: an examination to be taken after a minimum of three years of practice in a full-time public school teaching position. This test would measure: 1) subject-matter competency; 2) knowledge of learning theory, i.e., ability to diagnose accurately student needs in terms of skill level and social development and to match those needs with appropriate learning experiences, materials, and methods; 3) ability to monitor progress of students in a systematic way, utilizing several feedback mechanisms; 4) ability to create well-balanced lessons that vary activities and build progressively from facts to concepts to valuing and evaluating, thus giving students opportunities for and experiences in raising their thinking and reasoning skills; and 5) ability to evaluate accurately student progress in a manner that is consistent with stated goals and objectives and that involves students as active participants in the evaluation process.

Such a test would be to teaching what the Certified Public Accountant's examination is to accounting. As such, it would be entirely voluntary. Only those who wished to take the test for purposes of professional advancement would do so. It is also strongly recommended that the test be made optional on a nationwide basis. This would have the added benefit of opening up the job market for master-level teachers. Outstanding educators who find themselves in dead-end positions in their own school districts could seek advancement not only outside their districts, but also outside their states. Such open competition would work for the benefit of all concerned. Areas experiencing growth would have an excellent pool from which to select, while teachers who were seeking advancement in their careers would not have to leave teaching in order to progress professionally. These master-level teachers would be compensated accordingly, just as CPA-level accountants are.

Of course, individual states and local school districts could supplement that national examination with locally designed sections, reflecting state concerns and priorities. For example, a state with a large limited-English-speaking pupil population might want to emphasize the importance of teachers being expert in this area, while other states might emphasize other areas of great need.

TEACHER EDUCATION REFORMS

In addition to promoting teacher professionalism by encouraging and rewarding teachers who have objectively demonstrated superior skills as educators, the introduction of a CPA-like examination for teachers would also place teachers and the general polity in a more strategically advantageous position to press colleges and universities to undertake reforms that would improve the educational enterprise at all levels. In particular, teachers and policy makers would have the leverage to persuade the higher education establishment to think more systematically about the process of teaching (knowledge transmission) and learning (knowledge acquisition) in particular disciplines (Gifford & Stoddart, 1985).

Traditionally, disciplinary departments (e.g., departments of physics, English, and mathematics) have not directed many of their resources or energies toward the examination of how students learn specific subject matter, what difficulties they face in learning how to think abstractly, what preconceptions they bring with them to the classroom, what instructional approaches are most effective for particular types of students, and how best to take full advantage of the potential of computer-based intelligent tutoring systems. The very promise of a CPA-like exam for teachers, covering what teachers should know about teaching and learning in particular subject areas, would vastly improve the linkages between teachers in the schools and teachers in colleges and universities. Here again, the American Association of Colleges 1985 report, "Integrity in the College Curriculum," speaks truth to established wisdom:

> If departments, particularly research departments, allocated one or two regular faculty positions to research on learning their discipline, they could produce results which would improve their own teaching effectiveness and would have visibility and impact beyond the walls of their own institutions. They would influence instructional materials at the secondary as well as the college level. And they could educate young researchers who would continue the enterprise and propagate it to institutions where it does not yet exist. (p. 16)

Conclusion

During the transitional period toward the implementation of this proposal, it is undeniable that there will be disappointment for those who fail teacher competency tests. However, given the proper use of well-constructed, correctly standardized measures, tests for prospective teachers are necessary for the development of the teaching profession and beneficial to the education of our young. If there is indeed a national commitment to quality education for all, as a part of our dedication to the principles of equality, then suggestions to change the requirements to fit the present median performance of minority teacher candidates will be ignored. Rather, the desired performance level will be retained, valid and unbiased tests will be developed, and minority students will be provided with the kinds of support and training that will make it possible for them to garner the learning and experience needed to pass the examinations for entry into and exit from teaching credential programs. The know-how to do all this exists; all that is needed now is to affirm the belief that a quality system of education will be attained only when there is equality of outcome in basic skills across economic as well as racial lines.

Teaching, the transmission of thought from one mind to others, of traditions and values from one generation to the next, is one of the most important activities of the human race. It is the one skill whose absence prevents magnificent successes and guarantees startling failures. Lacking good teaching, genius is struck dumb, poverty is made permanent, power is likely to be brutal, and culture doomed to be channeled into mind-forged ruts. Lack of teaching results in squabbling, atomistic tribes, each one pursuing narrow objectives, unable to identify with the aspirations of anyone outside of the group. Good teaching enables and ennobles, providing society with the tools necessary for self-perpetuation and self-renewal. To put forth the argument that minority youngsters, the most disadvantaged of the poor, and the least able to emancipate themselves from their impoverished surroundings, should be taught by our less-than-best teachers is to stand the idea of justice on its head. As admirable and important as is the goal of increasing the ranks of minority teachers, this objective must not be put before the more fundamental objective of securing good teaching for those who need it the most.

References

Allen v. Alabama State Board of Education, 612 F. Supp. 1046 (M.D. Ala. 1985), vacated February 4, 1986.

American Association of Colleges. (1985, February 13). Integrity in the college curriculum. *The Chronicle of Higher Education, XXXI*, 1-30.

Anrig, G. R. (1986). Teacher education and teacher testing: The rush to mandate. *Phi Delta Kappan, 67*, 447-451.

Brott, R. (1983). *Testing teachers*. Berkeley: University of California, Policy Analysis for California Education.

California Commission on Teacher Credentialing. (1984). *CBEST performance in relation to personal background factors*. Sacramento: Author.

California Postsecondary Education Commission. (1984). *Response to request from state board of education regarding the screening of applicants to teacher education programs*. Sacramento: Author.

Cronin, J. M. (1983). State regulation of teacher preparation. In L. S. Shulman & G. Sykes (Eds.), *Handbook of Teaching and Policy* (pp. 171-191). New York: Longman.

Cross, L. H. (1985). Validation of the NTE tests for certification decisions. *Educational Measurement Issues and Practices, 4*, 7-9.

Educational Testing Service. (1983a). *Guidelines for proper use of NTE tests*. Princeton, NJ: Author.

Educational Testing Service. (1983b). *NTE programs: Core battery and specialty area tests*. Princeton, NJ: Author.

Edwards, H. (1983, August). Educating black athletes. *The Atlantic Monthly, 252*, 31-38.

Gallegos, A. M. (1984). The negative consequences of teacher competency testing. *Phi Delta Kappan, 65*, 631.

Gallup, A. (1984). The Gallup poll of teachers' attitudes toward the public schools. *Phi Delta Kappan, 66*, 97-107.

Gifford, B. R. (1984a). *The good school of education: Linking knowledge, teaching and learning*. Berkeley: University of California, Graduate School of Education.

Gifford, B. R. (1984b). Prestige and education: The missing link in school reform. *Education Review, 10*, 186-198.

Gifford, B. R. (1985). Teaching—from occupation to profession: The sine qua non of educational reform. *New England Journal of Policy Analysis, 1*, 60-75.

Gifford, B. R. (1977). *Race, ethnicity and equal employment opportunity: An investigation of access to employment and assignment of professional personnel in New York City's public schools.* New York: Board of Education of the City.

Gifford, B. R., & Stoddart, T. (1985). Teacher education: rhetoric or real reform? In P. Johnson (Ed.), *Education on trial: Strategies for the future* (pp. 177-198). San Francisco: Institute for Contemporary Studies.

Goertz, M., & Pitcher, B. (1985). *The impact of NTE use by states on teacher selection.* Princeton, New Jersey: Educational Testing Service.

Hoffman, B. (1962). *The tyranny of testing.* New York: Collier Books.

Ivie, S. D. (1982). Why black students score poorly on the NTE. *High School Journal, 65*, 171.

Mercer, W. A. (1983). Teacher education admission requirements: Alternatives for black prospective teachers and other minorities. *Journal of Teacher Education, XXXV*, 26-29.

Nairn, Allan & Associates. (1980). *The reign of ETS: The corporation that makes up minds.* Washington, DC: Learning Research Project.

National Commission on Excellence in Education. (1983). *A nation at risk: The imperative for education reform.* Washington, DC: U.S. Government Printing Office.

National Education Association. (1980). *Measurement and testing: An NEA perspective.* Washington, DC: National Education Association.

National Evaluation Systems, Inc. (1985). *The excellence of the Alabama teacher certification testing program.* Amherst, MA: Author.

Owen, D. (1985). *None of the above: Behind the myth of scholastic aptitude.* Boston: Houghton Mifflin Company.

Pugach, M. C., & Raths, J. D. (1983). Testing teachers: Analysis and recommendations. *Journal of Teacher Education, XXXIV*, 37-43.

Rebell, M. A. (1986, February 21). *Disparate impact of teacher competency testing on minorities: Don't blame the test-takers—or the tests.* New York City: Rebell & Katzive, Attorneys at Law.

Scherer, M. (1983). Who's afraid of teacher competency tests? *Instructor 92*, 49-60.

Shanker, A. (1985). A national teacher examination. *Educational Measurement: Issues and Practice, 4,* 28-31.

Smith, G. P. (1984). The critical issue of excellence and equity in competency testing. *Journal of Teacher Education, XXXV,* 7.

Stoddart, T., Losk, D. J., & Benson, C. S. (1984). *Some reflections on the honorable profession of teaching.* Berkeley: University of California, Policy Analysis for California Education.

U.S. Department of Education, Planning and Evaluation Service, Office of Planning, Budgeting, and Evaluation. (1986). *State education statistics: Student performance, resource inputs, and population characteristics 1982-1985.* Washington, DC: U.S. Government Printing Office.

Vold, D. J. (1985). The roots of teacher testing in America. *Educational Measurement Issues and Practice, 4,* 5-7.

Watkins, Richard W. (1985). *Third year passing rates on the California Basic Educational Skills Test (CBEST) and passing rates by institution attended.* Sacramento: California Commission on Teacher Credentialing.

Weaver, W. T. (1984). Solving the problem of teacher quality, part 1. *Phi Delta Kappan, 66,* 108-115.

Footnote

1. The Alabama remedy is based on the court settlement in *Golden Rule Insurance Company v. Washburn, et al.,* No. 419-76 Ill. Circ. Ct. 7th Jud. Circ., November 12, 1984. In the *Golden Rule* case, it was determined that there were unacceptable differences in the performance of blacks and whites on the Illinois Licensing Exam for insurance brokers. The settlement required the test to be revised. Items where blacks scored as well as whites, within 15 percentage points, were to be included in the new test prior to items on which the performance differential was greater.

Testing Reform in California

Linda Bond

This chapter briefly reviews the recent history of testing in California. There has been an evolution over the last nine years. The experts can let the state know whether, in their opinion, California is still struggling to get up on the shore, whether it is standing upright, whether it is using the right tools, and, if it is using any tools at all, whether it is using them correctly.

The First Wave: Pupil Proficiency

The first wave of the recent evolution began in 1977, when Gary Hart, a state assemblyman (now a state senator), carried a bill on pupil proficiency tests. His interest derived from his own classroom experience. Fresh-faced, idealistic, perhaps naive, as a first year high school civics teacher he was asked, at the last minute, to teach a geography class as well. He was obliged to rely on the textbook until he realized that a number of the students in his class could not read.

He did not know what to do, and he approached a senior colleague who said, "You don't understand the system here. If a kid shows up and doesn't disrupt the class, he gets a passing grade." Hart went along with that system, reluctantly. He felt, thereafter, and still feels that he and other teachers did a disservice to those youngsters.

LEGISLATION

When he was elected to the legislature in 1974, Hart put together a pupil proficiency testing bill before this approach was as popular as it is today. It was somewhat of a surprise to him that the idea got as much attention as it eventually did. In the process he asked the testing industry whether valid tests in the basic skills could be developed by or for local school districts, and if so, what those tests might measure. He was told, straightforwardly, that there were valid tests in reading, writing, and mathematics.

Do these proficiency tests that are in place measure important reading, writing, and math skills? Are they valid for that purpose?

Linda Bond is Special Consultant to the Senate Committee on Education, California State Legislature.

California believes they are. Are they valid for determining whether a student has performed well in high school? Are they valid as a measure of student performance in high school? Absolutely not.

The Second Wave: Teacher Competency

The second wave resulted from the first. As in other states, the pupil proficiency law led to a concern about the competency of the teachers in the classroom. For students there was a sanction, the pupil proficiency law, that said if one did not master basic proficiencies, if one did not pass the test, one did not get a diploma. Many parents and students in turn came to Gary Hart and said, "We can understand the proficiency test for students and even the denial of a diploma, but if you want us to accept that, then give us teachers who are literate."

Hart responded in 1981 by putting together teacher competency legislation, knowing that the vast majority of California teachers were indeed literate and much more. There were, however, individuals entering the system who had not mastered the basic skills of reading, writing, and mathematics. The bill passed and a test was developed with some help from teachers on an advisory committee. Does that test measure competency in basic skills appropriate for teachers? California thinks it does. Does it measure or predict teacher performance in the classroom? Absolutely not.

The Third Wave: Higher Order Credentialing

The third wave involves a more sophisticated set of tests and assessments for teacher certification. Albert Shanker, president of the American Federation of Teachers, testified before the California Commission on the Teaching Profession. He argued that a basic literacy test is not what California is looking for in ultimately establishing standards for the teaching profession. The standard must be one in which people can take some pride, a standard that actually helps attract people to teaching.

We determined that in some respects California had not been using tests enough. In this state, certification involves a set of courses and a state agency count of units and course titles. There is no accountability measure for teaching certificate candidates beyond state program approval. On the other hand, as California moves into a new phase in the evolution of testing, there is the risk of too great a reliance on tests.

COMMONS COMMISSION

As of April 1986, newly proposed legislation (Senate Bill 1605), being carried by Marian Bergeson, was part of a reform package, the other bill having been introduced by Gary Hart. Both bills are based on the recommendations of the California Commission on the Teaching Profession, called the Commons Commission after its chairman, Dorman L. Commons. The commission comprised 17 individuals who were selected because they do not represent any particular constituency.

Their major product was a report entitled *Who Will Teach Our Children? A Strategy for Improving California Schools.* The report incorporates 15 months of deliberation, a review of 17 commissioned research papers, written testimony from educators and lay citizens across the state, and observations during a series of school visits. The commission report made 27 interrelated recommendations, a number of them bearing on teacher certification and calling for a new system with three components.

GENERAL KNOWLEDGE

First, there should be assessment of general knowledge prior to entry into a teacher preparation program. This need not be a paper-and-pencil test; the idea is that the assessments would be developed by the institutions of higher education. The state's role would be to encourage these institutions to develop rigorous assessments across a variety of subject areas.

SUBJECT MATTER

The second component would be a standardized test in a subject-matter field. The test would be taken as a part of the credentialing process, a series of steps that this chapter cannot include. These standards are to be developed by a new state credentialing board composed primarily of teachers. The report continually stresses the importance of involving teachers in these decisions.

With the new subject-matter tests, the CBEST (California Basic Education Skills Test), which is currently the basic literacy test for teachers, would be repealed and replaced with more complex, sophisticated subject-matter exams.

SITE VISITS

The third and most important component would be a series of on-site assessments. Each beginning teacher would enter a "residency," a prolonged internship experience. The individual would enjoy a reduced teaching load, but with full pay, and would have support from a mentor teacher, a colleague-coach. There would also be opportunities to meet with other teachers and to gain the benefit of their insights and advice. During the residency, there would be a series of reviews by a higher education faculty member, the teacher's supervising administrator, and senior teachers who are experts in the subject area as applied at a particular grade level.

BASIS OF PLAN

The commission based its recommendations on a number of assumptions. First, new tests must be developed; current tests will not do the job. Second, new tests can provide a valid measure of subject-matter knowledge. Third, new tests cannot provide a valid measure of teaching methods and effectiveness, contrary to the claims of some.

A Perspective on Testing

In testimony to the commission, some researchers claim that a test can adequately measure pedagogical skills, provided that the exam includes a simulation. They claim that such tests would be valid, cost efficient, time efficient, and "clean" (objective, not influenced by the subjective views of administrators). The commission, however, did not accept these claims. Instead it placed substantial emphasis on on-site assessments, modeled on residencies in other professions. The on-site assessments are seen to provide a high degree of local school board control and "ownership"; they encourage a high degree of involvement by local teachers and administrators. Most importantly, they move away from a checklist mentality in teacher evaluation toward more complex reviews of teacher performance by experts, mainly other teachers.

Even if research clearly showed that standardized testing of teacher performance was valid, the commission would not have found that approach preferable to in-class observation. We can identify elements of the knowledge base in teaching, such as subject matter, pedagogical theory, child psychology, and measurement.

Nonetheless pedagogical testing, at best, can assess only what a teacher knows about learning theory and child development, not what the teacher can do. Tests do not take into account qualities essential to effective performance: motivation, perseverance, patience, and sensitivity. Ironically, in view of the present rush toward testing, standardized tests of pedagogy do not provide assurance that the teacher in fact can perform in the classroom. Therefore, the commission recommended subject-matter tests coupled with on-site assessment.

A Challenge

This chapter closes with an agenda and perhaps a challenge. First, all of us who are involved in education, particularly the testing experts, should speak out about the benefits and the limitations of tests. Second, we should all work for a major restructuring of the teaching profession. Accountability measures are only one element of needed reform. In order to attract caring, competent people to teaching, we need significant changes in school management, in teacher roles and responsibilities, and most importantly, in teacher working conditions.

Third, the profession must expand the knowledge base in teaching and develop new tests that can accomplish limited but valid purposes. Tests can play a significant role in enhancing the pool of teacher candidates and improving the status and compensation of teachers.

Finally, and most importantly, educators need to resist the efforts of ambitious politicians who tend to seize upon the testing issue. Such efforts may be well intentioned, but lack of knowledge regarding the limits of testing ultimately will be destructive to efforts toward improving the quality of education in this country. Only by resisting ill-conceived efforts can we assure continuing evolution in testing and, therefore, improved effectiveness.

Legal and Technical Design Issues for the Examination for the Certification of Educators in Texas (ExCET) Program

William Phillip Gorth
Barbara C. Appel
Jeanne W. Clayton

The ExCET Development Procedures

This chapter presents the development process for the Examination for the Certification of Educators in Texas (ExCET) program in relation to four major technical and legal issues: validity, reliability, bias, and standard setting. The paper discusses the purpose of teacher licensure tests and presents the major technical and legal context of these tests. The discussion relates these issues to a series of legal precedents, indicating how the developmental process for the Texas project reflected those issues.

Purpose of Teacher Licensure System

The primary purpose of teacher licensure testing and the provision of teaching certificates is to protect the public. "Licensing requirements are imposed to ensure that those licensed possess knowledge and skills in sufficient degree to perform important occupational activities safely and effectively" (American Education Research Association, American Psychological Association, & National Council on Measurement in Education, 1985, p. 63). By regulating the entry of individuals to the teaching profession, state education agencies carry out their responsibility to protect the public, particularly children in school.

BENEFITS

Teacher licensure testing provides a basis for improving the quality of education. Teacher applicants who are not yet competent

William Phillip Gorth is President of National Evaluation Systems, Inc.
Barbara C. Appel is an Area Director for Licensing and Certification at National Evaluation Systems, Inc.
Jeanne W. Clayton is an Area Director for Licensing and Certification at National Evaluation Systems, Inc.

are screened out. By providing diagnostic information, the tests also allow not-yet-competent individuals to improve their content knowledge and ready themselves to enter the classroom.

Teacher licensure testing has other benefits as well. By defining acceptable levels of performance for entering teachers, the testing program increases the clarity of state education requirements for local districts and schools of education. Support materials such as study guides and score report interpretive manuals link the test to learning objectives and help strengthen the statewide curriculum. Score reports to schools of education alert the institutions to the problems their students may be having, both individually and in aggregate, with the areas of content measured by the test and taught in public school classrooms, thus informing their process of curriculum review and revision.

Major Technical and Legal Issues

Any licensure program should evidence sensitivity to the guidelines of various professional agencies and federal laws, regulations, and court decisions, where applicable. The legal interpretation of these guidelines in a specific project is probably best done by legal counsel. This chapter, therefore, should not be viewed as legal advice but should be seen as raising topics for discussion in specific situations. The Equal Employment Opportunity Commission (EEOC) *Federal Uniform Guidelines and Employment Selection Procedures* (1978), adopted also by the Civil Service Commission, U.S. Department of Labor, and U.S. Department of Justice, and the *Standards for Educational and Psychological Testing* (1985), prepared by the American Educational Research Association (AERA), the American Psychological Association (APA), and the National Council on Measurement in Education (NCME), recommend certain procedures in developing licensure tests. These technical and legal guidelines are reviewed for the four fundamental aspects of test development: (1) validity, (2) reliability, (3) bias, and (4) standard setting.

VALIDITY

Section 3 of the EEOC *Guidelines* (1978) states that any employment test that has an adverse impact on any minority group may be considered discriminatory unless the validity of the test has been shown.

> The use of any selection procedure which has an adverse impact on the hiring, promotion, or other employment or membership opportunities of members of any race, sex, or ethnic group will be considered to be discriminatory and inconsistent with these guidelines, unless the procedure has been validated in accordance with these guidelines. (p. 82)

Section 4D regards adverse impact as occurring generally whenever the selection rate for a minority group is less than four-fifths of the group with the highest rate.

> A selection rate for any race, sex, or ethnic group which is less than four-fifths (4/5) (or eighty percent) of the rate for the group with the highest rate will generally be regarded by the Federal enforcement agencies as evidence of adverse impact. (p. 98)

Section 5A of the EEOC *Guidelines* (1978) provides standards for conducting validation studies.

> For the purposes of satisfying these guidelines, users may rely upon criterion-related validity studies, content validity studies or construct validity studies, in accordance with the standards set forth in the technical standards of these guidelines. (p. 104)

Section 14C(1, 4) states that content validity studies are appropriate if the selection procedure is based on a representative sample of the content of the job. There remains some question as to how directly applicable this section is to licensing situations.

> Users choosing to validate a selection procedure by a content validity strategy should determine whether it is appropriate to conduct such a study in the particular employment context. A selection procedure can be supported by a content validity strategy to the extent that it is a representative sample of the content of the job. . . . (p. 158)

> To demonstrate the content validity of a selection procedure, a user should show that the behavior(s) demonstrated in the selection procedure are a representative sample of the behavior(s) of the job in question or that the selection procedure provides a representative sample of the work product of the job. (p. 162)

Section 14C(2) states that content validity studies should include a job analysis.

> There should be a job analysis which includes an analysis of the important work behavior(s) required for successful performance and their relative importance and, if the behavior results in work product(s), an analysis of the work product(s). Any job analysis should focus on the work behavior(s) and the tasks associated with them. If work behavior(s) are not observable, the job analysis should identify and analyze those aspects of the behavior(s) that can be

observed and the observed work products. The work behavior(s)
selected for measurement should be critical work behavior(s) and/or
important work behavior(s) constituting most of the job. (p. 162)

The AERA/APA/NCME *Standards* (1985) include a primary
standard (11.1) for the content validation of professional and
occupational licensure and certification tests. "The content domain
to be covered by a licensure or certification test should be defined
clearly and explained in terms of the importance of the content
for competent performance in an occupation" (p. 61).

It is stated in the Comments section for this standard that "job
analyses provide the primary basis for defining the content domain"
(p. 64).

LEGAL PRECEDENTS

The courts have attended to these suggested practices in a
number of cases. The EEOC *Guidelines* (1978) are sometimes seen
by program administrators as having force of law, stemming as
they do from Title VII of the 1964 Equal Employment Opportunity
Act. In fact, it is not clear that they apply to licensing tests, as
distinct from employment tests. As the reader will note in the
following review, most of the cases that cite the *Guidelines* do not
involve licensing situations.

Specifically, several cases have indicated the importance of the
job relatedness of test content in substantiating the validity of a
test. The absence of a job analysis study in *Albemarle Paper Co.
v. Moody* (1975) contributed significantly to the Supreme Court's
decision to hold the test as valid. A similar impact can be seen in
United States v. City of Chicago (1977) and in *Kirkland v. New York
Department of Correctional Services* (1974).

Moreover, the courts have indicated (e.g., in *Easley v. Anheuser-
Busch, Inc.*, 1983) that the job analysis should explore the relative
importance of the job components so that the resulting test can
reflect those differences or perhaps exclude job elements that may
be a part of the job but are unimportant or not essential.

One can identify a number of other dimensions that the courts
have used to evaluate the validity of testing programs. These
include whether the evaluation criteria are related to well-defined
job characteristics and requirements or are based on some sort
of overall review. The courts have shown a distinct preference for
the former.

RELIABILITY

The second critical guideline that should be considered in developing a teacher licensure test is reliability, or the degree to which test scores are free from errors of measurement. Section 14C(5) of the EEOC *Guidelines* (1978) deals with reliability. "The reliability of selection procedures justified on the basis of content validity should be a matter of concern to the user. Whenever it is feasible, appropriate statistical estimates should be made of the reliability of the selection procedure" (p. 164).

The AERA/APA/NCME *Standards* (1985) include estimates of reliability as a primary standard (Standard 11.3). "Estimates of the reliability of licensure or certification decisions should be provided" (p. 65). The developer of licensure and certification tests is also referred to a general standard (2.1) for providing reliability estimates.

> For each total score, subscore, or combination of scores that is reported, estimates of relevant reliabilities and standard errors of measurement should be provided in adequate detail to enable the test user to judge whether scores are sufficiently accurate for the intended use of the test. (p. 20)

For whatever reason, there are few court cases that cite reliability statistics as a problem in a testing program probably because the computation of such data is a standard aspect of almost all testing programs. Also, it is difficult to argue how technical deficiencies in reliability statistics relate to adverse impact.

BIAS

The third critical issue to be considered in developing a teacher licensure test is prevention of bias. The EEOC *Guidelines* (1978) state that an employment test that has adverse impact may be considered discriminatory unless its validity is established. Therefore, ensuring that the test covers the appropriate content domain is an important step in preventing bias.

Besides ensuring the validity of the test, the test developer should also be alert for bias in individual items. The *Standards* (AERA et al., 1985) address this issue in Chapter 3, "Test Development and Revision."

> When selecting the type and content of items for tests and inventories, test developers should consider the content and type in relation to cultural backgrounds and prior experiences of the variety of ethnic, cultural, age, and gender groups represented in the intended population of test takers. (p. 26)

In the Comments section for this standard, it is suggested that
". . .test developers might establish a review process using expert
judges both to select item material and to eliminate material likely
to be inappropriate or offensive for groups in the test-taking
population" (p. 26).

It is further suggested that:

> At various points in test development, empirical procedures may
> be needed. Such procedures may be needed, for example, when
> constructing interest inventories, in which differential item response
> rates may exist for different gender, ethnic, and educational groups.
> Differential response rates do not necessarily invalidate such items
> or scales based on them. However, the developer's aim should be
> to maximize scale validity and, within this constraint, the developer
> should strive to minimize the potential misrepresentation of interests
> for major groups in the population that is served. (p. 26)

It is obvious to any observer that analysis of methods undertaken
to eliminate bias has played a role in court decisions for many
testing programs. The language of the courts varies. In some
situations, the focus is on the general validity of the testing
instrument. In others, the wording addresses the generalizability
of the validity (i.e., is the test equally valid for all population groups
affected by the program?). In most teacher certification testing
situations, the groups are limited to whites, blacks, and Hispanics.
The body of decisions include these as well as cases involving
gender-based differences that are not typically at issue in teacher
testing.

As noted above, the major protection against a charge of
discrimination is afforded by a sufficiently validated test and a
developmental process that includes adequate documentation and
procedures. This chapter does not attempt a comprehensive review
of relevant cases. We refer the reader to other sources including
Nathan and Cascio (1987). Among the better known and most
directly applicable are *United States v. South Carolina* (1977) in which
the courts upheld the National Teachers Examination for
certification purposes and *Bridgeport Guardians v. Bridgeport Police
Department* (1977) in which the use of a police hiring test was
upheld as valid despite adverse impact on blacks.

STANDARD SETTING

If passing (cutoff) scores are used, Section 5H of the EEOC
Guidelines (1978) requires that "they should normally be set so as
to be reasonable and consistent with normal expectations of
acceptable proficiency within the work force" (p. 114).

Many different procedures have been established for setting cutoff or passing scores. Whatever procedure is chosen, it should be technically sound and clearly documented. The *Standards* (AERA et al., 1985) deal with this issue in Chapter 10, "Employment Testing": "A clear explanation should be given of any technical basis for any cut score used to make personnel decisions" (p. 62). As is the case in most of the other areas discussed in this chapter, legal decisions apply primarily to employment testing situations rather than to licensing tests.

The EEOC *Guidelines* (1978) and AERA/APA/NCME *Standards* (1985) provide useful guidelines to consider when developing licensure tests that are valid, reliable, and free of bias, and have cutoff scores that are technically sound. The Elliot et al. chapter in this book describes the developmental process of the ExCET test in relation to several of these issues.

Discussion Issues about the ExCET

The major goal of the test development process for the ExCET was to create a set of 34 tests, each of which had professionally acceptable psychometric qualities in conformity with legal and professional standards. These are validity, reliability, bias, and standard setting. In this section of our chapter, we highlight the portions of the development process that most contributed to the psychometric characteristics of the tests.

Validity

Validity is considered, by most educational researchers and by the courts, as the primary characteristic of a test or testing program. However, validity is not an "all-or-none" characteristic; rather, it is present in degree and depends upon the range of information collected to support the particular use of the test.

PSYCHOMETRIC STANDARDS
The two works that served as general guidelines during the developmental procedures were the EEOC *Guidelines* (1978) and the AERA/APA/NCME *Standards* (1985). Both documents were considered in planning the overall structure of the project.

Both sources focus test development procedures on the job to be performed by the individual who is to be tested. Thus, the *content* of the job is to provide the content for the test, and the relationship is the basis of the validity of the instrument. In discussing content validity, the EEOC *Guidelines* (1978) state that a test should measure a representative sample of the content of the job. The definition of the job of a licensed teacher practicing in Texas requires the consideration for any of the job assignments that an individual with a license may hold. Therefore, the definition of the job must be structured to include a range of specific job assignments.

DEFINITION OF THE JOB

The license to teach (which in education is called the certificate) provides an individual with opportunities to work in a variety of school settings, usually in teaching different grade levels and a range of content. Many states, Texas included, issue certificates that cover grades K-12 or 7-12 in a given discipline with all the variation that implies. Therefore, defining the job characteristics requires a process that takes into account this diversity.

Rebell (1986) has indicated that the information necessary to define a teacher's job may conceptually be drawn from at least three major sources, each discussed below.

STATE-MANDATED CURRICULUM

Texas has provided its elementary and high schools with substantial structure by defining curriculum content and instructional materials appropriate for public classrooms. The state has adopted specific objectives for courses in most subjects and grade levels. Further, the state provides for the systematic review and formal adoption of instructional material in most content areas. Both the Essential Elements of the Curriculum (the prescribed curriculum) and the adopted textbooks form a legal requirement for which teachers are responsible. The teacher certification tests, which are designed to measure an individual's knowledge of the subject area, should, therefore, consider this source of information about job content.

INFORMATION FROM INCUMBENTS

A survey of job incumbents is a traditional strategy for obtaining information about a job. As noted above, the range of job positions available to a person with a specific teaching certificate may be wide. The procedure to collect information is thus made more challenging because of the need to capture the diversity included under any given certificate. This information, gathered in Texas by means of surveys, contributes to the understanding of the relative importance of various components of content used by teachers with a particular certificate.

PROFESSIONAL PREPARATION

Third, the curriculum that is taught in teacher education programs reflects what some professionals in the field consider important content associated with a particular license. The teacher education curriculum provides a useful starting point and potential "test of completeness" for the content to be measured on the licensing test.

As indicated in the Elliot et al. chapter, the development process for the ExCET incorporated all three sources of content validity information. Briefly, these included a review of adopted textbooks in the state and the Essential Elements of the Curriculum requirements, a survey of teaching incumbents in each certificate field, and a survey of both teacher education faculty and students regarding the content of their training programs.

CROSS-CHECKING VALIDITY

The development process also included an independent verification of the content validity of the tests. Once the initial test development was completed, the tests were reviewed by an independent panel of content experts in each test field. The panel was asked to provide detailed information concerning the appropriateness of each test question for use in a certification program, both in terms of its match to the objective that was created at the beginning of the test development process as well as in terms of tasks expected of teachers in Texas. (If an item was judged not valid by a panelist, the panelist was asked to provide information that could be used to modify the item to make it valid for future use.)

Bias Prevention

Preventing bias was integrated into the entire test development process. First, the process was open; many educators, selected to be representative of the population groups and regions of the state, contributed. The process incorporated teacher education course content, programs of study, and instructional materials approved, after a detailed legal process, by the State Board of Education. Thus, the development process itself focused on the content domain that was widely reviewed and acknowledged as appropriate for educators in Texas. This constitutes a major step toward the prevention of bias in the tests.

Potential bias was an explicit category of review for all materials at all stages of development. The job analysis survey generated empirical data from a random sample of teachers in each subject-matter field. As indicated earlier in the discussion of the legal cases, establishing the validity of the instrument is a critical aspect of a successful defense against claims of bias. Clearly, the survey contributes to that defense by linking test and job content.

The field tryout data were analyzed in terms of differential performance of ethnic and gender groups to identify whether or not items had characteristics requiring further review. In addition to this empirical information, each item was individually reviewed for bias, both by the test development advisory committees and the content validation/standard setting committees. Last, a separate panel of reviewers independently reviewed the test items specifically and solely from the standpoint of potential bias in the development process.

Conclusions

Developing 34 tests for use in a teacher certification program for Texas demanded procedures that would handle the many requirements for licensing and would deal with the diversity of the teaching fields in the state. The Texas Education Agency and National Evaluation Systems, Inc., worked together to create the development process as described elsewhere in this volume.

Checks and balances were incorporated at many points throughout that process. Important test attributes, such as validity, were established for the test through a variety of developmental steps that allowed knowledgeable professionals to provide input at many stages in the process and provided a verification by an independent group of educators. Such checks and balances, combined with the empirical data from the surveys of teachers, teacher educators, and education students, provided the assurances necessary that the program would meet professional standards.

References

Albemarle Paper Co. v. Moody. (1975). 422 U.S. 405.

American Educational Research Association, American Psychological Association, & National Council on Measurement in Education. (1985). *Standards for Educational and Psychological Testing.* Washington, DC: Author.

Bridgeport Guardians v. Bridgeport Police Department. (1977). 431 F. Supp. 931.

Easley v. Anheuser-Busch, Inc. (1983). 572 F. Supp. 402; 758 F.2d 251.

Equal Employment Opportunity Commission, Civil Service Commission, U.S. Department of Labor, & U.S. Department of Justice. (1978). Adoption by four agencies of uniform guidelines on employee selection procedures. *Federal Register, 43,* 38290-38315.

Kirkland v. New York State Department of Correctional Services. (1974). 374 F. Supp. 1361; 520 F.2d 420.

Nathan, B. A., & W. F. Cascio. (1987). Technical and Legal Standards for Performance Assessment. In Berk, R. (Ed.), *Performance Assessment: Methods and Applications.* Baltimore: Johns Hopkins University Press.

Rebell, M. A. (1986). Legal Issues in Test Validation. In National Evaluation Systems, *Practical Issues in Teacher Certification Testing.* Amherst, MA: Author.

Rebell, M. A. (1985). Recent Legal Issues in Competency Testing for Teachers. In Gorth, W. P., & Chernoff, M. L. (Eds.), *Testing for Teacher Certification* (pp. 59-73). Hillsdale, NJ: Lawrence Erlbaum Associates.

United States v. City of Chicago. (1977). 549 F.2d 415, cert. denied. 434 U.S. 875.

United States v. South Carolina. (1978). 445 F. Supp. 1094, aff'd. 434 U.S. 1026.

Setting Standards for the Examination for the Certification of Educators in Texas (ExCET)

Paula M. Nassif
Sharon L. Downs
Martin B. Karlin

Overview

Setting standards for the Examination for the Certification of Educators in Texas (ExCET) program is a multifaceted process. Though the actual activity occurs as the final step in test development, standard setting is supported by all previous program activities. The process relies on the consistency of previous definitions of program design, development, and materials review. For example, the tests are designed to measure entry-level content or pedagogy skills, to be job related, and to assess competence at a minimum level. This goal provides the context for reviewing other project activities so that the final materials (i.e., test items) are consistent with the overall program design.

Background

Most cutoff-score techniques used today have their origins in the traditional procedures developed earlier by Nedelsky (1954) and Angoff (1971). Berk (1986) identified 38 methods for setting standards. The procedures he catalogs involve judgment-based systems, empirical approaches, and processes that combine judgment and test result data. Each technique has its unique advantages and associated problems. There are considerable similarities among them because of the common roots many share in the Nedelsky and Angoff procedures.

Paula M. Nassif is Vice President for Research and Operations at National Evaluation Systems, Inc.
Sharon L. Downs is an Area Director for Licensing and Certification at National Evaluation Systems, Inc.
Martin B. Karlin is an Area Director for Licensing and Certification at National Evaluation Systems, Inc.

NEDELSKY

One popular approach for setting standards was originally developed for use on examinations in medicine. The Nedelsky (1954) approach is flexible: test length does not matter, normative data are not necessary, and the number of judges or raters can vary.

MODIFIED NEDELSKY/ANGOFF

A procedure employed by National Evaluation Systems, Inc. (NES) (Nassif, 1978) is a straightforward, dichotomous version of Nedelsky (1954), used originally for setting standards on teacher licensing tests in Georgia. This procedure matches closely that described in Angoff (1971). In this approach the entire item, rather than each distractor, is examined and classified in terms of its "necessity" for meeting the minimum skill level required for a given purpose. Statistical significance of agreement among judges is determined by comparing the number of judges rating an item as "necessary" with criteria established by probability tables for the binomial distribution. The total number of items judged as "necessary" becomes the initial passing, or cutoff, score.

In order to account for errors in measurement, the minimum cutoff score determined by expert judges may be adjusted by subtracting the standard error of measurement. This adjustment of the cutoff score due to measurement error has been supported in *South Carolina Education Association et al. v. State of South Carolina et al.* (1977).

ANGOFF

In the approach commonly referred to as the Angoff approach (1971), an entire test item is reviewed and judged against the probability that it will receive a correct response from a person of minimum competency. Like the modified Nedelsky approach, Angoff's procedure is less time consuming than Nedelsky's (1954), because each judge reviews the item in its entirety, rather than by its component parts.

The modified Nedelsky and Angoff (1971) procedures for setting cutoff scores are similar in concept and in practice. Both rely on expert judges; both are item-based; both proceed item-by-item, reviewing each item in its entirety; both may or may not include empirical performance data; and both are composed of independent judgments. Also, the question asked of the judges, which serves as the basis for determining the cutoff score, is conceptually quite similar in the two techniques. In the modified Nedelsky model, the judge is asked "whether a person with minimum competence ought to be able to respond to the item correctly"; response is dichotomous (yes or no). In the Angoff method, the judge determines "the probability that the minimally acceptable person would answer the item correctly."

JAEGER

Jaeger (1978) developed an iterative approach that allows judges who carry out the standard-setting approach to review the results of preliminary standard setting and revise their judgments based on this information.

After an orientation to the standard-setting task, each judge receives a copy of the test, completes it, and is told the correct answer for each item. Judges then make a recommendation on each test item by answering questions about whether the candidate should be able to answer the item correctly. Then the judges answer the following question: "If a candidate does not answer this item correctly, should (s)he be denied a certificate?"

The cutoff, or passing, score, defined as the number of items that a judge indicated should be answered correctly, is calculated for each judge, and a histogram of the passing scores suggested by a given group of judges is presented to that group. In addition, judges are given statistics that indicate the percentage of examinees who answered each item correctly during the field test. Each judge reviews the items again, developing a new set of decisions based on this additional information.

Passing scores are computed again and histograms are distributed. With this new information, judges make a final determination of the "necessity" of each item as a certification requirement. Final distributions of passing scores are determined and reported to the judges.

If more than one type of judge (e.g., classroom teachers vs. teacher educators) is involved, the passing scores for each category are pooled and the median is computed. The final passing score takes into account the median rating for each group of judges.

This approach has been applied with some modification to the validation of a teacher licensing test in North Carolina (Cross, Impara, Frary, and Jaeger, 1983).

The Texas Model

The standard-setting process used in Texas systematically collected judgments from professional educators, summarized them, and reported them to the State Board of Education as a partial basis for the determination of the passing score for each test. The approach combines features of both the Angoff (1971) and Jaeger (1978) models. The Texas process involved the use of field test data, item-by-item ratings from judges working independently, and a two-stage review that provided judges with an opportunity to reconsider their item-by-item ratings based on information regarding the range and averages of all judges' ratings.

In the Texas model, as in Angoff's approach (1971), judges provide estimates of the probability that a minimally competent person would answer each question correctly. The Texas procedure also incorporates several aspects of Jaeger's model, primarily the multiple, independent ratings by judges and the use of empirical field test data. Information used or provided during the first set of ratings is summarized for use during the second round.

VALIDITY

The collection of standard-setting data is related to the validity of each test question in that only questions rated as valid by judges will have standards associated with them. Similarly, only content that is familiar to the majority of judges will have standards associated with it. Judges were not asked to rate items covering content they did not know themselves.

RATIONALE

In a licensing environment, determining the passing score for tests is critical. The consequences of classification errors are serious both for individual examinees and for the pupils they will eventually instruct. The seriousness of the responsibility normally requires that the State Board of Education, as the highest policy-making body, establish the final cutoff scores. In fact, this was to be the procedure in Texas. The state board would review both the preliminary recommendations of the Texas Education Agency (TEA), which were based on information from the standard-setting panels, and the results of the initial administration of the ExCET. Only then would the cutoff scores be finalized.

Procedure in Texas

The list on the following page indicates the general flow of standard-setting procedures in Texas. In all of the steps, judges work independently.

Round One:

1. Review of individual test items.
2. Review of field test data on individual items.
3. Rating of individual test items.

Round Two:

1. Review of mean judges' ratings from step 3.
2. Second rating of individual test items (judges could retain or revise their original rating).

Final:

1. Final compilation of results from all judges in a given field.

JUDGES

The content-expert judges who set preliminary standards for each test included faculty members from teacher training institutions in Texas and currently certified and practicing Texas teachers in each field. The TEA selected between 8 and 12 educators per field to participate in the standard-setting activities.

Each of the educators received background material about the ExCET program and a detailed agenda of activities during the two-day process. The first day included an extensive orientation and training session. The training session comprised detailed descriptions of project background information, extensive explanations of the standard-setting process, specific instructions on how to complete the forms and materials, and a procedure for ensuring that all questions from judges were answered satisfactorily and in a standardized way across all groups. Each content-expert judge received a training manual, an item review booklet, field test data forms, machine-scannable answer sheets, objectives with content annotations, project background description sheets, practice session materials, test security forms, confidentiality sheets, personal information forms, and item comment forms.

ROUND ONE—ITEM-BY-ITEM RATINGS

After reviewing the test items, each judge was asked if he or she was familiar with the content measured by each item. If the judge was unfamiliar with the content, no more judgments were made on that item. The diversity of most content fields makes it likely that any one judge may be less familiar than another with the content of some specific questions. It does not seem reasonable for a judge to review or recommend standards for an item under those circumstances. Next, the judge rated the validity of each item. Rating an item affirmatively meant that the item:

- matched the objective,

- was accurate,

- was free from bias, and

- represented knowledge used to perform the job of an entry-level educator in Texas.

CONTENT VALIDATION

The panel members also participated in an independent content validation of the test items. Each panel member evaluated the items in his or her subject-area field for accuracy, match to the objective, and absence of potential bias.

While reviews of this type had already been completed by the advisory committees, this second review enhanced the validation process for the test. The standard-setting panels had had no prior role in the program and, hence, had no stake in the items. They could approach the items without any "history"; this independence is important. Moreover, a review of the items familiarizes participants with the materials before the standard-setting activities begin.

If a judge rated an item as "not valid," the reason for the rating (according to the four criteria above) was recorded and no more judgments were to be made on that item.

For each valid item, each judge estimated what percentage of minimally competent individuals would answer the item correctly. In answering the question, "What percentage of entry-level educators who have the minimum amount of content knowledge necessary to teach acceptably in the state of Texas in their certification field would answer the item correctly?" judges were told to imagine a hypothetical group of individuals who have a minimum amount of content knowledge necessary to teach acceptably in Texas in their certification field. Judges were asked to rate each item as one of a range of percentages. For example, if a judge felt that between 0 percent and 10 percent of this minimally competent group would answer the item correctly, the judge would mark the scanning sheet with a "1." The correspondence table is on the following page. In short, an item that the judge thought "easier" (i.e., more minimally competent candidates could answer it correctly) would receive a higher score.

Rating Correspondence Table

Percent Estimated To Answer Correctly	Rating
0-10	1
11-20	2
21-30	3
31-40	4
41-50	5
51-60	6
61-70	7
71-80	8
81-90	9
91-100	10

Before a judge recorded the rating, he or she reviewed the data summary to get an indication of the percentage of the examinees who answered the item correctly during the field test. Judges were reminded that this percentage reflected all examinees, not just minimally competent examinees, and that some fields contributed a relatively small number of participants, so that field test data should be interpreted with caution. Judges were asked to rate each item independently of other items and not to be concerned with how many items were rated at any given point on the percentage scale.

Judges participated in practice activities before beginning their task. There was group discussion on all ratings for each sample item. Throughout the training process, judges were referred to specific sections of the training manual and were given opportunities to review the instructions, ask questions, and demonstrate their understanding of the procedures.

In completing their ratings, judges were instructed to go back through their booklets to assure that they had rated all items to reflect current opinion.

Following these rating activities, NES staff ran various data analyses, using microcomputers and optical scanning equipment. The second round reviews all included use of the ratings generated during round one.

ROUND TWO—ITEM-BY-ITEM RATINGS

At the start of the second day, each judge received statistical analyses, provided as computer printouts, containing for each item:

- the item identification number,

- the range of ratings given by all raters,

- the median rating of all raters, and

- the judge's own rating.

In round two, each judge reviewed each item that he or she deemed "familiar" in round one and that the group had consensually determined to be valid. Judges considered their colleagues' median ratings and score ranges and responded again to the question, "What percentage of entry-level educators who have the minimum amount of content knowledge necessary to teach acceptably in the state of Texas in their certification field would answer the item correctly?" They were neither encouraged to change nor discouraged from changing their ratings, but they were asked to consider their ratings in light of the additional information provided. Judges recorded their round two judgments on a separate response sheet.

Two points deserve emphasis here. First, if the consensus among judges in a given subject-matter field was that an item was not valid, that item was either dropped or revised to reflect the comments made by the judges. Second, the iterative nature of this review and the incorporation of empirical data (judges' ratings) borrow significantly from the Jaeger (1978) approach as summarized earlier in this chapter.

The use of judges' ratings in the reconsideration of standards by individual judges enhances the consensual nature of the resulting recommended standards. As implicit in all standard-setting procedures, professional judgment is a universal feature. One of the major assets of the Texas approach is its incorporation of reviews of pooled judges' ratings.

Results

The overall results of the content validation indicated that over 99 percent of the items were judged valid through the collective ratings of all individual judges. Of the items judged as valid, each item had a unique standard associated with it for the compilation of the preliminary cutoff score in the first operational test form. Because of the confidential nature of this information, specific results cannot be disseminated.

References

Angoff, W. H. (1971). Scales, norms, and equivalent scores. In R. L. Thorndike (Ed.), *Educational measurement* (2nd ed.) (pp. 508-600). Washington, DC: American Council of Education.

Berk, R. A. (1986). A consumer's guide to setting performance standards on criterion-referenced tests. *Review of Educational Research, 56,* 137-172.

Cross, L. H., Impara, J. C., Frary, R. B., and Jaeger, R. M. (1983). *A comparison of three methods for establishing minimum standards on the National Teachers Examination.* Paper presented at the annual conference of the American Educational Research Association.

Jaeger, R. M. (1978). *A proposal for setting a standard on the North Carolina High School Competency Test.* Paper presented at the annual meeting of the North Carolina Association for Research in Education.

Nassif, P. M. (1978, March). *Standard-setting for criterion-referenced teacher licensing tests.* Paper presented at the annual meeting of the National Council on Measurement in Education, Toronto.

Nedelsky, L. (1954). Absolute grading standards for objective tests. *Educational and Psychological Measurement, 14,* 3-19.

South Carolina Education Association et al. v. State of South Carolina et al., Civil Action No. 75-1610, District of South Carolina (1977).

References

Validating the Examination for the Certification of Educators in Texas (ExCET)

Scott M. Elliot
Kathleen M. Cole
Deborah F. Magid

Establishing test validity of any teacher licensing program involves both technical considerations (American Educational Research Association [AERA], American Psychological Association [APA], & National Council on Measurement in Education [NCME], 1985) and legal guidelines (Equal Employment Opportunity Commission [EEOC], Civil Service Commission, U.S. Department of Labor, & U.S. Department of Justice, 1978). This chapter describes the specific procedures used in validating the Examination for the Certification of Educators in Texas (ExCET).

The Gorth et al. chapter in this volume provides an overview of the technical and legal considerations in establishing the validity of teacher licensing tests. We refer the reader to that comprehensive discussion.

Texas Validation Approach

One of the primary concerns in designing the ExCET program was test validity. The test development process was designed to meet both legal requirements and professional standards (as reflected in the AERA/APA/NCME *Standards* [1978] and relevant literature on validity). There are several key features to the validation approach designed for the ExCET program:

- validation procedures at each step in the test development process
- multiple sources of validity evidence
- consistency with Texas public policy
- empirical links to Texas educational practice
- use of advisory committees

Scott M. Elliot is Division Director for Licensing and Certification at National Evaluation Systems, Inc.
Kathleen M. Cole is a Project Director in the Division of Licensing and Certification at National Evaluation Systems, Inc.
Deborah F. Magid is a Project Manager in the Division of Licensing and Certification at National Evaluation Systems, Inc.

VALIDATION AT EACH TEST DEVELOPMENT STEP

The validity literature (cf. Cronbach, 1971; AERA et al., 1985) emphasizes that validation is a process of accumulating evidence in support of a test rather than a single event at one point in time. While many test development efforts rely on a single validation procedure (typically post hoc), the decision was made at the outset of the ExCET program to include validation procedures at each step in the test development process. Steps to ensure validity were taken in defining the test domain, conducting the job analysis, developing item specifications, and constructing items. Moreover, a separate, independent validation of test items was conducted.

MULTIPLE SOURCES OF EVIDENCE

Any single source of validity evidence could be called into question. To ensure the validity and defensibility of the ExCET tests, multiple sources of validity evidence were obtained at each step in the process. The major sources were Texas public policy and Texas educational practice.

TEXAS PUBLIC POLICY

The state of Texas has enacted a great deal of legislation and board of education policy relating to education. There are state-mandated curricula that define what must be taught in the various subject areas in public schools, state-adopted textbooks that are approved for use in the classroom, and formal standards for teacher preparation programs. These aspects of policy were actively incorporated into the test development process in order to ensure that the test would be valid specifically for Texas teachers. The Texas statutory codes, approved textbooks, representative course syllabi from teacher education programs, and other materials provided by the Texas Education Agency (TEA) all served as source materials to develop the ExCET tests.

TEXAS EDUCATIONAL PRACTICE

Both the EEOC *Guidelines* (1978) and AERA/APA/NCME *Standards* (1985) speak to an empirical link between the content of the job and the domain of the test. To ensure that the ExCET tests reflect educational practice in Texas, a systematic job analysis of practicing public school teachers was conducted. As a further source of information about educational practice in the state, teacher educators and teacher education program students familiar with Texas teacher requirements were surveyed to verify the students' exposure to the content to be tested.

USE OF ADVISORY COMMITTEES

As a further measure to ensure that the ExCET tests reflect educational practice in Texas, the TEA convened for each certification field an advisory committee composed of Texas educators from both public schools and higher education institutions. The committee was responsible for reviewing materials at each step in the test development process.

ExCET Validation Procedures

The test development process for the ExCET program consisted of nine major steps.

1. *Domain Definition*—specifying the domain of content in the form of measurable objectives.

2. *Job Analysis*—determining the set of objectives taught or used on the job.

3. *Objective Selection*—identifying a representative sample of job-related objectives to be tested.

4. *Development of Item Specifications*—delineating the content to be measured within each objective and identifying appropriate measurement strategies.

5. *Item Development*—developing test items to measure the content specified.

6. *Field Tryout and Review*—collecting empirical data to determine the preliminary performance of test items under actual testing conditions.

7. *Bias Review*—assessing whether or not the items and the test as a whole contained any bias.

8. *Content Validation*—establishing the validity of test items through review by an independent panel.

9. *Standard Setting*—establishing a passing score for each test.

Domain Definition

Both the EEOC *Guidelines* (1978) and the AERA/APA/NCME *Standards* (1985) indicate that the domain measured by licensing tests must clearly reflect the domain of the job. Several measures

were taken to ensure that the definition of the ExCET tests
represented the job as reflected in Texas public policy and practice.

OBJECTIVE DEVELOPMENT

The State Board of Education Rules for Curriculum (TEA, 1984a)
and other requirements for educational practice contained in the
Texas Education Code were the starting point for identifying the
job-related content and selecting a meaningful way to structure
content for each test field. These materials were supplemented by
a review of state-adopted textbooks, TEA curriculum guides, the
State Board of Education Rules for Teacher Education (TEA, 1984b),
and curriculum materials used in approved teacher preparation
programs in Texas.

OBJECTIVE CODING

A coding system was used to document the source or sources
of specific content for each test; each objective was coded to one
or more state policy or curriculum documents. The coding system
provided documented evidence that the objectives defining the test
domain were matched to the sources defining the content taught
or used on the job.

As a final validity check before their consideration by the advisory
committees, the outlines and objectives were reviewed both by
practicing teachers and by curriculum specialists at the TEA.

REVIEW AND REVISION OF THE TEST OBJECTIVES

In January 1985, committees comprising practicing teachers and
teacher educators from across the state met to review the test
outlines and objectives.

The purpose of this review was to evaluate the organization and
inclusiveness of test outlines and objectives as they related to the
job of teaching in a Texas public school classroom. Committee
members reviewed the objectives for their significance, accuracy,
level of specificity, taxonomic level, lack of bias, relevance to entry-
level teachers, and appropriateness for assessing minimum content
knowledge required for the job.

OBJECTIVE MATCH TO THE RULES FOR CURRICULUM

After the committee recommendations had been implemented,
test objectives were reviewed by National Evaluation Systems, Inc.
(NES) and recoded to the Rules for Curriculum (TEA, 1984a), where
necessary. The final sets of objectives and coding information were
then reviewed and verified by TEA curriculum specialists. The

major purpose of this coding was to ensure that the test objectives remained clearly linked to the Rules for Curriculum. In all cases, all of the Rules for Curriculum for a given certificate area were matched to one or more objectives on the test.

Job Analysis

Consistent with the EEOC *Guidelines* (1978) and AERA/APA/NCME *Standards* (1985), a systematic job analysis of Texas educators was conducted. The job analysis was carried out to obtain empirical data on the degree to which each of the test objectives in each teaching field reflected what a practicing teacher uses or needs to know on the job in Texas. Surveys were also mailed to teacher candidates and teacher educators to obtain information on the extent to which the content of the test objectives was presented to teacher candidates either before or during their teacher preparation programs.

TEACHER SURVEY DATA COLLECTION

For the job analysis, a random sample of certified, practicing teachers was selected to review and rate the test objectives in each field. On the average, the sample size for each test field was 300 teachers. For each objective, respondents were asked to indicate if they used or taught the content of the objective. For each objective used or taught, they were instructed to indicate how much time they spent teaching or using the objective in comparison to other objectives, and how important they felt the objective to be to the job. Responses to the question of time spent teaching or using an objective were rated on a five-point scale ranging from "very little time" to "very much time." The importance of the objective to the job was also rated on a five-point scale ranging from "no importance" to "very great importance."

The overall response rate for the job analysis of public school teachers was 79 percent.

TEACHER SURVEY DATA ANALYSIS

The results of the teacher job analysis were analyzed to determine the extent to which the objectives were used on the job and considered important to the job.

The following analyses were conducted:

- the distribution of responses on the demographic questions

- the percent of educators teaching or using the content of each objective

- the mean job analysis rating for time spent teaching or using the content of each objective, the standard deviation of the mean, and the standard error of the mean

- the mean job analysis rating for importance of the objective to the field, the standard deviation of the mean, and the standard error of the mean

- a scatterplot of mean ratings of time spent by mean ratings of importance

In addition to these analyses, an index of job relatedness was developed by combining the time spent and importance ratings through the formula:

$$\sqrt{(\text{mean time spent})^2 + (\text{mean importance})^2}$$

The formula yields a convenient, common reference for committee members reviewing the job analysis results.

TEACHER EDUCATOR AND STUDENT SURVEY DATA COLLECTION

The purpose of the student and teacher educator samples was to provide additional information about the extent to which the objectives were related to the teaching job in Texas. On the average, 100 students and 100 teacher educators were sampled per field. Students were asked to respond to the question, "Have you ever received instruction in the content of this objective either before college or as part of your college education program?" Teacher educators were asked, "Do you teach the content of this objective in your courses OR expect that students would know the content of the objective for your courses?" They were also asked to rate the importance of the objective for the field on the same five-point scale used in the job analysis of public school teachers.

The student data provided information on the proportion of students receiving preparation in the content of each objective. The teacher educator data provided a corroborative measure of student preparation as well as a mean rating of importance. These measures in addition to the job analysis data were considered by the advisory committees in selecting the final sample of objectives to be measured on the tests. They constitute a form of "curricular validity" (i.e., examinees did have an opportunity to learn the content of the objective during their regular educational program). While curricular validity is not considered significantly important in teacher certification testing, the program benefits by having this additional check.

The overall response rate for the student sample was 50 percent; the rate for the teacher educator sample was 51 percent.

The analyses from the teacher, teacher educator, and student surveys were summarized on an Objective Classification Form as follows:

- Objectives for each major content area of the test were listed in descending rank order based on the general (combined) index of job relatedness from the teacher survey.

- Objectives receiving a mean index of job relatedness rating of less than or equal to 2.83—*and* not related to a state mandate for curriculum or practice—were considered to be outside of the job domain for the test.

- Objectives that 10 percent or fewer of the respondent teachers reported that they used were flagged for committee consideration.

- Objectives that the majority of students responding to the survey indicated that they had not received instruction for were flagged for committee consideration.

- Objectives that the majority of teacher educators responding to the survey indicated that they did not expect students to know the content of were flagged for committee consideration.

- Objectives for which the mean importance rating by teacher educators was less than or equal to two (i.e., considered of little or no importance) were flagged for committee consideration.

Objective Selection

The EEOC *Guidelines* (1978) state that the content of a licensing test should reflect a representative sample of the important content of the job. In June 1985, test development advisory committees met to select the sample of job-related objectives representative of the job domain. To accomplish this task, committee members used the Objective Classification Form which provided a rank ordering of objectives within the major subareas of each test based on the results of the job analysis survey. The complete data analysis from the job analysis survey was also available to committee members.

Based on the job analysis, the advisory committees selected a representative sample of objectives for test development. The committees selected a number of objectives to be tested in proportion to their numbers within each major content subarea for the field.

Development of Item Specifications

To delineate further the specific elements of Texas public policy and practice to be measured on the ExCET, detailed item specifications and general test specifications were prepared in each test area. The development of these specifications for the ExCET program required a thorough and systematic review of state-adopted textbooks, curriculum guides, teacher preparation course materials, and relevant public laws from the state of Texas as a means of building content validity into the tests. The purpose of this review was to identify the most significant aspects of each objective and begin to judge the relative emphasis that should be given to each aspect.

The results of this literature review were presented to the test development advisory committees. The test specifications addressed general considerations that were applicable to the test as a whole. They included:

- a description of the format in which items for the field were to be written,

- basic item-writing guidelines,

- general content specifications (e.g., definitions or symbolic conventions used), and

- sample items.

The individual item specifications:

- delineated aspects and characteristics of the content of each objective to be tested,

- indicated methods for measuring specific aspects of content,

- listed assumptions, where relevant, about the domain of the objective, and

- indicated instances where special emphasis should be placed on one or more of the aspects of the objective.

A sample of item specifications appears on the following page. The specifications are for a fictitious field and are meant to indicate

SAMPLE

Examination for the Certification of Educators in Texas
Field (Number and Name)

ITEM SPECIFICATIONS

Subarea: (Title)
Cluster: (Title)
Objective: (Number)

Synergistic Objective: Understand the basic principles of contract law.

Content Limits:
1. Define terms related to contracts.
2. Analyze components or characteristics of various types of contracts.
3. Apply the principles of contract law to a given situation.

Content Specifications: Terms related to contracts may include express contract, implied contract, offer, acceptance, counteroffer, firm offer, voidable, material facts, duress, undue influence, consideration, detriment, forbearance, seal (*locus sigilli*), parol, assignment, novation, release, breach, tender of performance, discharge, execution, etc. Items may involve identifying definitions, synonyms, or examples.

Components and characteristics may refer to the necessary requirements or elements (e.g., agreement, competent parties, legal purpose) for forming and executing various types of contracts (e.g., valid, voidable, implied at law, under seal). Analyses may involve the relationships between contractual elements, cause-effect relationships, missing elements, and successful or unsuccessful execution of a contract.

Applications of principles may involve applying any of the above items or principles to a given real or hypothetical situation.

Comments: Examples and situations should be brief, realistic, and easily understandable (avoid legal jargon). Situations may relate to more than one item.

Emphasis: The focus should be on applying basic principles of contract law to common situations (e.g., sales contracts, employment contracts). Avoid exceptions and legal technicalities.

the general nature of those used in the ExCET program. They differ from the type of specifications used by other test developers but serve well the purpose of making clear the content of the test questions to both committee reviewers and item writers.

The advisory committee members reviewed the item specifications for their match to objectives, significance, content coverage, difficulty level, accuracy, and freedom from bias. These criteria mirrored those used in the objective development and helped to maintain the link to job-related knowledge and skills.

Item Development

The item specifications provided detailed guidelines on the specific elements of Texas public policy and practice to be measured by the test items. All participants in the item-writing process were provided with the test specifications, item specifications, detailed guidelines for writing and reviewing test items, and all Texas materials identified in the item specifications.

As a final review before presentation to the advisory committees, classroom teachers and subject-matter specialists reviewed the complete set of items for their teaching fields to ensure that each item and the items as a whole were accurate, represented important content knowledge, and were relevant to a classroom teacher's job.

In October 1985, the test development advisory committees met to review the test items. The criteria used at this review included:

- match to objective,
- representation of important aspects of the objective,
- relation to knowledge needed on the job as a teacher in a Texas public school classroom,
- appropriate level of difficulty,
- content accuracy, and
- freedom from bias.

The advisory committees revised items as necessary based on these criteria to ensure that the items were appropriate for the certification of entry-level teachers.

Field Tryout and Review

In December 1985, NES conducted a field tryout to determine if the items developed exhibited expected statistical characteristics using standard criteria for evaluating criterion-referenced licensing and certification tests. More than 5,000 students in Texas teacher education programs participated across the 34 test fields.

The criteria used to evaluate items included:

- Item Difficulty—if 40 percent or fewer of the examinees answered the item correctly, the item was flagged for further review.

- Item-Total Test Reliability—if the point-biserial correlation for item-total test reliability was less than or equal to .10, the item was flagged for further review.

- Item-Objective Reliability—if the point-biserial correlation for item-objective reliability was less than or equal to .20, the item was flagged for further review.

Approximately 20 percent of the items were flagged for further review by the test development advisory committees based on the field test item analyses. In reviewing the field tryout results and flagged items, the committees attempted to identify possible causes for each item's performance characteristics. Considerations included item clarity, difficulty, significance, and bias, as well as the goals of the testing program. Items were revised where appropriate.

For the purpose of the review of field test results, classical statistical criteria were most appropriate. There was no attempt at this point in the project to assemble test forms, and hence no concern with equating forms. The field test review was done on an item-by-item basis, using information that met both professional statistical standards and that was accessible to the committee. Committee members were trained in interpreting the field test results.

Bias Review

JUDGMENTAL REVIEW

The purpose of the bias review was to ensure that test items were appropriate for all groups regardless of sex, race, age, religion, socioeconomic status, or regional background. Although freedom from bias was a criterion used in every stage of the development process, an independent minority panel was convened in January 1986 to examine items specifically and exclusively for bias. Panel members were provided with empirical data on differential performance collected during the field tryout where sufficient numbers of minority group members were available for analysis. (In some fields there were not enough minority candidates to generate reliable statistical information.) The test development advisory committees had also reviewed test data using group performance differences as a criterion.

The bias review panel was responsible for:

- reading through the entire bank of objectives and items for the field to become familiar with the content covered by the test and to ensure that the bank, taken as a whole, represented a variety of perspectives with regard to sex, race, and ethnicity where items required treatment of such characteristics;

- reviewing all items, together with the field tryout summary data for subgroups, to determine if they contained any language or content that would disadvantage or offend any group because of sex, race, ethnicity, age, religion, socioeconomic status, or regional background; and

- identifying items they felt were biased and recommending ways in which the items could be revised to eliminate the bias.

STATISTICAL REVIEW

In addition to the field tryout data broken down by subgroup, Angoff Transformed Item Difficulties (1971) were computed for those fields in which there were at least 25 members of two or more comparison subgroups. Items in which the difference in delta values between comparison groups was greater than or equal to 1.5 times the standard deviation of the delta residuals were flagged for specific scrutiny.

The bias review served to address both test validity and item validity for subgroups within the population as well as for the target population as a whole. The subgroup comparisons involved men and women and whites, blacks, and Hispanics (wherever sufficient numbers of field test participants were available).

Content Validation

In February 1986, an independent content validation was conducted to verify the validity of each item for each field. A new panel of Texas educators was convened in each field to independently review the test items. The size and composition of these panels of expert judges mirrored that of the original test development advisory committees.

The content validation committee members had an opportunity to familiarize themselves with the content and structure of the field as a whole as well as the content and structure of the test bank before beginning the task of judging items. Each item was then rated on a dichotomous scale (valid/not valid) for content validity using several criteria:

- Does the item match the objective for which it was written?

- Is the item accurate?

- Is the item free from bias?

- Does the item reflect content necessary for the job?

At least 51 percent of the judges had to rate an item valid for the item to be eligible for inclusion on the test. Items that any judge rated invalid were reviewed and verified against source documents after the conference to ensure their validity; if their validity could not be ensured, such items were declared ineligible for use on the test.

The major benefit of this step is the additional assurance provided by having an independent review of all test items. The individuals serving on the panels had had no prior involvement in the project. They brought with them an entirely fresh perspective and no "stake" in the items and objectives.

Standard Setting

The final step in the test development process was to collect information from the content validation committees that could be used to recommend to the State Board of Education a preliminary standard for each of the tests. The purpose of the standard-setting procedure is to determine at what level an examinee must perform on the tests in order to be judged minimally competent to practice in the Texas public schools.

The specific standard-setting procedures that were used are described in the Nassif et al. chapter in this book.

Summary

At each step in the test development process, multiple checks were made to ensure the validity of the tests. Validation is a complex process that demands the use of multiple sources of evidence. The many sources used in the development of the ExCET program represent a concerted and systematic effort to ensure their validity.

References

American Educational Research Association, American Psychological Association, & National Council on Measurement in Education. (1985). *Standards for educational and psychological tests.* Washington, DC: Author.

Angoff, W. H. (1971). Scales, norms and equivalent scores. In R. L. Thorndike (Ed.), *Educational Measurement* (2nd ed.) (pp. 508-600). Washington, DC: American Council on Education.

Cronbach, L. J. (1971). Test validation. In R. L. Thorndike (Ed.), *Educational Measurement* (pp. 443-507). Washington, DC: American Council on Education.

Equal Employment Opportunity Commission, Civil Service Commission, U.S. Department of Labor, & U.S. Department of Justice. (1978). Adoption by four agencies of uniform guidelines on employee selection procedures. *Federal Register, 43,* 38290-38315.

Texas Education Agency. (1984). State Board of Education rules for curriculum. *Texas Education Code* § 21.

Texas Education Agency. (1984). State Board of Education rules for teacher education. *Texas Education Code* § 137.

The Legal, Political, and Historical Basis of the Examination for the Certification of Educators in Texas (ExCET) Program

Marvin Veselka
Pamela Tackett

Advisory Committee Background

As a number of other states implemented certification testing programs in the 1970s, Texas was beginning to examine a full range of issues related to the quality of education offered by the public school system. In 1979, Governor William P. Clements, Jr., established the Governor's Advisory Committee on Education. The committee's report advised that competency testing of teacher education students could offer greater assurance of higher standards of intellectual, academic, and professional quality in individuals certified as public school educators. It recommended that the state establish a testing program for persons seeking initial certification that would assess competency in academic skills, knowledge of subject matter in the teaching field, and proficiency in the skills of teaching.

The Commission on Standards for the Teaching Profession was created by the legislature during the same period the governor's committee was reviewing the status of education. The commission was composed of 16 teachers, administrators, and teacher educators. It accepted the report of the governor's committee and began its own deliberations. The commission requested position papers from all areas of the profession on minimum competency testing prior to full certification. Requests were mailed to every school district, presidents of all of the professional education organizations in Texas, the state education service centers, deans and heads of colleges and schools of education, and many other interested individuals and groups. Maximum effort was made to circulate information about the commission, its meetings, and its intent and efforts, and to receive input from all affected individuals.

Marvin Veselka is Associate Commissioner for Professional Support, Texas Education Agency.
Pamela Tackett is Program Director, Texas Education Agency.

Seven public hearings occurred, during which 106 groups offered testimony and 250 presentations took place. In addition, the audiences at each hearing filled out questionnaires.

After a year, the commission issued its *Report and Recommendations on Classes and Duration of Certificates and Competency Testing of Teachers*, which made two recommendations:

(1) All degreed persons seeking initial teacher certification in Texas should submit scores on subject area examinations in areas for which certification is requested.

(2) The Commission on Standards for the Teaching Profession should continue to study and identify appropriate examinations on teaching methodology.

The State Board of Education accepted the commission's report, incorporating these recommendations into the board's message to the session of the legislature that began in January 1981.

Implementing Legislation

In the spring of 1981, the Texas legislature passed Senate Bill 50, dealing specifically with teacher certification testing. The statute stated:

... the board by rule shall require satisfactory performance after graduation from an in-state or out-of-state teacher education program on a comprehensive examination prescribed by the board as a condition to full certification as a teacher and shall require satisfactory performance on a separate examination prescribed by the board as a condition to certification as a superintendent or other administrator. The board shall prescribe an examination designed to test knowledge appropriate for certification to teach primary grades and an examination designed to test knowledge appropriate for certification to teach secondary grades. The secondary teacher examinations must test knowledge of each examinee in the subject areas listed. . . . (Part C, SEC. 1, Section 13.032(e))

In the fall of 1981, the State Board of Education began to adopt the rules that would implement the statute. The rules called for the first test administration in the spring of 1986, providing protection for students who were already pursuing teacher certification. The 1986 date placed the incoming freshman class in the fall of 1982 on notice that, upon graduation, certification requirements included successful performance on both subject-matter and pedagogy tests.

Initial Program Formulations

Progress on the implementation of the legislative mandate for initial certification testing was slow in the beginning. The Commission on Standards and the State Board of Education carefully studied the issue before deciding to develop state-owned tests rather than to use existing measures. During 1983, they approved a design that called for individual subject-matter tests in each of the specialization areas at the secondary level and a professional development or pedagogy test. At the elementary level, a comprehensive test covering the elementary curriculum would be accompanied by an elementary professional development test. The design also called for tests in other certification areas, such as counselor and administrator. In all, a battery of 64 tests was needed to cover the certificates awarded by the state of Texas.

ESSENTIAL ELEMENTS

The next major step was to determine a content framework for the tests. In the late 1970s and early 1980s, the back-to-basics movement was prevalent in Texas, as well as nationally. In fact, the legislature directed the repeal of all existing statutory requirements for curriculum and authorized the State Board of Education to establish a new curriculum for the public schools. The major content areas were dictated by statute. The board was to define the Essential Elements of the Curriculum of these content areas by grade level and course.

A vast number of educators were involved in the development and refinement of the Essential Elements, which were to describe the curriculum to be taught. Each school district would be required to provide instruction in the Essential Elements at the appropriate grade levels. School districts were given license to add elements, but they could not delete or omit instruction as required by the State Board of Education. The Essential Elements in the state-mandated curriculum became the foundation for determining the content of the certification tests. A detailed job analysis was planned and implemented, but emphasis was also placed on state curriculum requirements.

In 1984, the Texas Education Agency called for bids on the first of two phases (34 out of 64 tests) of test development in time for the initial administration in 1986. The process called for involving Texas educators in both elementary and secondary education and institutions of higher education in the development, review, and revision of the tests. National Evaluation Systems, Inc., of Amherst,

Massachusetts, won the contract in the fall of 1984 for both phases of test development and for test administration.

The full implication of certification testing in Texas is yet to be assessed, and its impact on the quality of teacher education will be reviewed in the coming years. There is evidence of heightened interest in curriculum changes on Texas college campuses, while Texas public schools are reviewing the testing requirements in light of the supply of teachers needed for the growing Texas school population.

References

Texas Senate Bill 50 (1981). *Texas Education Code* § 13.032.

Assisting Examinees and Teacher Education Programs in Preparing for the Examination for the Certification of Educators in Texas (ExCET) Program

Nolan Wood
Barbara S. Clements
Cherry L. Kugle

Program Goals

An effective teacher certification testing program must do more than simply categorize prospective teachers into "pass" and "fail" groups. The program must provide the support to assist teacher educators and examinees toward the end of improving classroom instruction. The Examination for the Certification of Educators in Texas (ExCET) program includes a variety of procedures aimed at evaluating examinees' specific knowledge and skills as required to provide instruction in Texas public schools. Elliot and Stotz (1986) explain how this information can be used:

> The knowledge and skills, which are stated as the performance objectives or competencies identified during test development, serve as instructional "targets" for the preparation of prospective teachers. These targets can be used by individuals because diagnostic test results identify their strengths and weaknesses and help remediate the latter. They can also help teacher preparation programs focus on job-related skills. (p. 269)

TEST STRUCTURE

The list of skills and specific knowledge required for each test in the ExCET program was derived from several sources of information and expertise. The Texas Education Agency (TEA) and its contractor, National Evaluation Systems, Inc. (NES), created a

Nolan Wood is Director of Teacher Assessment with the Texas Education Agency.
Barbara S. Clements is an Educational Specialist with the Texas Education Agency.
Cherry L. Kugle is an Educational Specialist with the Texas Education Agency.

preliminary set of objectives that defined the important content
in a test area. Sources included the state-mandated curriculum for
the test area (called the Essential Elements of the Curriculum),
public school textbooks, and teacher preparation program materials
(textbooks, syllabi, and course materials) solicited from teacher
educators in the 66 approved college and university programs in
Texas. For each test area, the TEA selected an advisory committee
consisting of six public school teachers or supervisors and four
college faculty members (two from teacher education programs
and two from academic departments). The advisory committee for
each test area reviewed and revised the objectives with the goal
of defining the field in terms of its most important content
knowledge and skills.

JOB ANALYSIS SURVEY

NES formatted the complete set of objectives for each test area
as a survey instrument and sent it to a sample of public school
teachers, teacher educators, and teacher education students in each
field. The job analysis survey sought information on the relevance
and importance of each objective and served as a preliminary
indication to teacher educators and teacher education students of
the content considered important for a test area. After reviewing
the results of the job analysis survey, the advisory committees
selected the subsample of test objectives that would be included
on each test. Thus, test content was affected by the three major
populations involved in the program.

FIELD TESTING

Field tests for each test area took place in December 1985.
Students in the final stages of teacher preparation were invited
to participate in the field tests for their areas of certification;
approximately 5,000 students from colleges and universities in
Texas participated. Teacher education faculty members assisted
in administering the tests and talked with students as they
completed the tests. The field tests thus enabled future examinees
to experience the actual test items and the scope of content included
in their certificate areas. In addition, faculty members had the
opportunity to learn more about the content and format of the
tests and to get student assessments of test difficulty.

INDEPENDENT VALIDATION

An independent validation committee for each test area was
selected to review proposed test items for content validity and to

recommend passing standards. The TEA created these committees to reflect the composition of the original advisory committees. Therefore, four additional college faculty members in each test area were included in the test development process.

While the TEA requested participants in the development of the ExCET tests to maintain the security of the selected objectives and actual test items, the teacher educators received significant amounts of general information that could be shared with colleagues concerning requirements for content knowledge that would be needed by all teacher education program graduates.

In short, the test development process afforded many opportunities for teacher educators to review test content. This review constituted an important source of information about the tests, information that teacher educators can use in preparing their students for the ExCET. Moreover, future examinees had an opportunity to take the test in their certification areas during the field test. The development process itself has been a meaningful form of support to those who are affected by program requirements.

Specific Support Materials

In addition to the information indigenous to the development process itself, the TEA undertook to create several specific documents aimed at providing support to examinees and teacher training institution faculty members. The ExCET program includes procedures for informing examinees and teacher educators of the purpose of the testing program, the content of each test, and suggestions for preparing for the tests. Preparation materials have been disseminated as rapidly as possible during the lengthy test development process.

ANNOTATED OBJECTIVES

Once final objectives defining the content of each test were available, NES annotated them to provide illustrative information concerning the content covered under each. Certification candidates are encouraged to familiarize themselves with the objectives for their areas of specialization early in their education programs. In this way they can select courses to ensure coverage of job-related content. In October 1985, the TEA sent lists of annotated objectives for ExCET test areas to deans and chairpersons of teacher education programs with instructions to make these lists available to students who would be required to take the tests. In addition, potential examinees were referred to the Essential Elements and state-adopted public school textbooks for further information in the content areas.

STUDY GUIDES

NES prepared a separate study guide for each test area to provide several types of information to potential examinees. The study guides contain general information about the ExCET program, suggestions for use of the study guides, and general test-taking strategies. The entire list of annotated objectives for a given field is included. In addition, there is a practice test of 20 sample questions representing 20 objectives. For each question, the objective and a rationale for the correct answer are provided. The practice test items derive from the pool of actual test items.

INFORMATION SESSIONS

The TEA has undertaken a variety of activities to explain the ExCET program to teacher educators and examinees and to help in the preparation of examinees. The TEA has participated in presentations to teacher educators and potential examinees at professional meetings and at sessions held on college campuses. A Network for Teacher Competency Testing has been created to help interested college faculty members and certification officers exchange methods and materials developed to prepare students for state-mandated testing programs and to provide remediation when necessary. As new study programs and materials are developed, the network will disseminate them to member institutions.

Summary

Teacher education programs are responsible for preparing certification candidates for positions in Texas public schools. One outcome of the ExCET program is the selection of content objectives that represent knowledge necessary to be an entry-level teacher in Texas as determined by public school educators and teacher educators who served on committees and participated in the job analysis survey and field test. This information will be used by teacher educators to ensure not only that beginning teachers can pass the required test, but also that they have the opportunity to learn the content they will need to be public school teachers.

References

Elliot, S. M., & Stotz, J. G. (1986). Teacher certification testing: Beyond regulation to instructional improvement. In W. P. Gorth & M. L. Chernoff (Eds.), *Testing for Teacher Certification* (pp. 267-276). Hillsdale, NJ: Lawrence Erlbaum Associates.

A Series of Brief Perspectives on Test Validity

Pascal Forgione, Jr.
Joan Brown
Joseph Robert Weaver
Nolan Wood
Robert Gabrys

This chapter comprises five statements concerning test validity in teacher certification. They were prepared by representatives of state agencies in Connecticut, the District of Columbia, Oklahoma, Texas, and West Virginia who are involved in such programs. Each brings to the topic a different perspective: going beyond content validity in teacher assessment by clarifying program targets; using content tests in combination with internships to strengthen teacher programs; influencing the quality of teacher preparation programs with test development and test results; creating a balance among inconsistent sources of test content; and developing tests based on the public school curriculum and job relatedness. These are not intended to be fully developed position statements, but rather brief, provocative reflections on aspects of validity for those agencies.

Pascal Forgione, Jr., is Chief of the Office of Research and Evaluation, Connecticut State Department of Education.
Joan Brown is Special Assistant to the Superintendent, District of Columbia Public Schools.
Joseph Robert Weaver is Director of Teacher Education, Testing, and Staff Development, Oklahoma State Department of Education.
Nolan Wood is Director of Teacher Assessment, Texas Education Agency.
Robert Gabrys is Director, Office of General and Professional Education, West Virginia Department of Education.

Content Validity Is Not Enough

Pascal Forgione, Jr.

In discussing educational leadership, it is important that a state is clear on where it is going and what the prevailing "political culture" is like, so that its plans for teacher assessment fit both the program goals and the political context. What works well for one state may not be appropriate for another. In Connecticut we have a history, for better or worse, of looking at a variety of testing options. The state periodically assesses students in science, social studies, mathematics, language arts, art and music, and business and office education. These assessments include applied and innovative activities such as the conduct of science experiments. Connecticut's tradition of reform in student assessment has set the tone for the teacher certification-related testing program; in fact, both assessment programs are run out of the same office. In initiating certification testing, we learned that it is possible to "move" the focus and targets of instruction across programs by clarifying what these targets are.

CONTENT VALIDITY

Based on Connecticut's assessment experience, we are not confident that content validity is enough to assure that the teacher examination incorporates the appropriate skills and subject knowledge that one believes teachers should have and be able to use. For example, can a teacher of mathematics bring the pedagogy to bear on the subject knowledge? Does the teacher know the knowledge misconceptions children bring with them and how to deal with those misconceptions? We believe that validity and credibility reside both in the quality of what we measure and in how we measure it, not simply in a demonstration that the existing test matches a narrow set of skills that can be measured in a paper-and-pencil format.

CREDIBILITY

The tests, to some extent, define our expectations for teachers. This is where Connecticut thinks the challenge lies: to bring credibility to the assessment so that a person who completes the certification assessment process feels that he or she has applied the reasoning and subject knowledge required of the job and has faced those processes and complexities that typify the classroom.

A major question resides in whether the research community is ready to assist state education agencies in this effort. In most states, the certification testing program is tied in with other reforms (e.g., higher salaries, a mentoring system). Connecticut's concern is that an exclusive focus on content validity without attention to criterion validity issues may trivialize what we are about.

In creating and administering our basic skills test for prospective teacher education students, we learned a lot about licensure. Connecticut is now proposing a two-stage assessment process. We will implement paper-and-pencil subject knowledge and literacy skills tests, a screen, for the some 5,000 people certified each year in Connecticut. These tests will not reveal how a teacher is going to perform in a classroom, but they will remove high-risk people from having an opportunity to teach without first correcting their deficiencies. That aspect of the tests meets a necessary state interest: to protect the health and welfare of Connecticut students.

Next, Connecticut is committed to implementing an in-depth clinical assessment as a part of a beginning-year teacher support and assessment program. Connecticut hires only about 1,000 new people a year. Our emphasis will be on a clinical assessment for those new teachers so that we can probe those essential subject-matter and pedagogical competencies that we could never expect to accomplish with a paper-and-pencil test. This is the real challenge for us and for the educational research community. We believe that we have to do more than concentrate on where we are now so that teacher assessment will move toward where we want it to be. In undertaking this approach, we hope the research community will help by investigating the issues and providing a solid foundation on subject and pedagogical knowledge that will contribute to a meaningful definition of teaching as a profession.

Testing within a Teaching Internship Program

Joan Brown

STAFFING STUDY

Major recent school reform in the District of Columbia dates from 1977. We instituted a competency-based curriculum in which all academic disciplines are outlined in a scope and sequence of learning objectives. In 1983, the District received a grant from Congress that asked us to study the issue of merit pay. The study was conducted by the Rand Corporation, and it helped the District to define as a goal the attraction, retention, and motivation of high-caliber teaching staff. We seek to attract bright, young people into the teaching profession, to retain those that we have, and to assemble all our various programs into an incentive package.

INTERN PROGRAM

An integral part of the District of Columbia Public Schools' intern program is the requirement that beginning teachers take subject-matter tests in their teaching fields. We do this even in the face of a staffing crisis. We know that by 1993, 50 percent of our teaching staff will have retired. The District's need for teachers will be substantial, and we must compete with surrounding counties that have similar needs and are recruiting vigorously. We are increasingly aware of this crisis of numbers, especially when we compete in the certificate fields of science, mathematics, foreign languages, special education, bilingual education, and early childhood education.

Our Board of Education has passed a resolution allowing a final decision in 1988 on the testing program for beginning teachers. District staff firmly believe that testing should be a part of a comprehensive program to help beginning teachers develop the knowledge and skills necessary to become successful professionals. We began with the development and validation of the testing program in December 1985 and will finish in December 1987. The first two classes of interns will comprise the pilot groups for test development. We will use their performance data to determine a cutoff score for each test. We will also use the results to decide whether to use the tests for certification and hiring or for granting tenure to teachers. Candidates who do not meet the cutoff score will be able to retake the test following appropriate professional development activities designed to address identified areas of deficiency. The tests will be criterion referenced and competency based, and will be tied to the objectives from our curriculum.

USING EXISTING MATERIALS

The District is adapting test objectives and items from the teacher certification testing program in Georgia. The Georgia materials have a long record of successful use. District staff studied Georgia's objectives carefully to assure ourselves of a match with our own written objectives. The first test administration was in May 1986. Examinees at that time were interns who had benefited from the services of mentors during the past school year. The mentors worked with the interns on the subject matter in the interns' teaching fields. These mentors have met standards and passed through a selection process developed by committees of teachers and the Rand Corporation. They are deemed exemplary, and they are supervising all beginning teachers. The mentors receive a stipend and additional training; they also participate in the evaluation of the intern.

The goal of the testing program is to improve the quality of teaching and learning in our schools by ensuring that our students have the best teachers that we can provide. We believe that the tests, in combination with the involvement of mentors, will move us toward that goal.

The Impact of the Testing Program
on Teacher Preparation

Joseph Robert Weaver

Oklahoma began development of its teacher certification tests in 1980. In 1977 we had initiated a process to reconstruct all of our certification programs and approved teacher education programs in our colleges and universities. These latter efforts did not reach maturity, however, until after certification tests were under development. In creating the certification tests, we utilized curriculum materials and textbooks that were being used in the state as a basis for the test objectives for a given content field. (It would have been helpful had there been a state-mandated curriculum in our public schools as a partial basis for development, as is the case in other states such as Texas and West Virginia.)

IMPACT ON TEACHER PREPARATION

The impact that the teacher certification testing program has had on the teacher education process is rather dramatic. The testing program was well under way before the new certification standards were begun. Hence, Oklahoma completed test development before the project on the certification standards was far along. The certification standards, consequently, reflect substantially the objectives of a particular test field (e.g., mathematics). The certificate programs are based almost entirely on the objectives that have been defined for the certification tests.

Teacher preparation institutions have taken the objectives for a given content test and have outlined elaborate matrices listing the objectives and the courses in their programs where these objectives are covered. Thus, we have seen a tremendous impact on teacher preparation from the teacher certification testing program. The testing program does not limit what the colleges teach; rather it provides an empirical definition of what common core knowledge prospective teachers in a given field must have.

Inconsistencies among Sources of Test Content

Nolan Wood

SPECIFYING CONTENT

When a test is developed, the specificity of content is critical. In teacher certification testing, the content must be job related, and demonstrably so. The Texas state-mandated Essential Elements of the Curriculum define required curricula and were one of the primary starting points in test development. A second source for test development was the *Texas Standards for Teacher Education,* passed in 1984 by the Commission on Standards. The *Standards* include rules that specify the subjects an individual may teach if he or she holds a given certificate. Our test objectives, therefore, had to reflect all of these frameworks: the Essential Elements, the teacher education standards, and the certification standards, as well as university curricula.

We found many inconsistencies among these sources. The major problem was with the Essential Elements, which lacked clarity and were ambiguous in many cases, and which contained both broad concepts and specific behaviorial objectives. In addition, we found that there were really two sets of certification standards, a written set and an unwritten set. In some cases, the certification standard did not match the area for which we were developing a test.

These problems are balanced somewhat by the fact that in 1988 Texas will be revising its state-based curriculum. Our experience with the first set of Essential Elements taught us where we made mistakes, especially because of an incomplete and imperfect understanding of the impact the Essential Elements would have on other programs within our educational system.

HIGHER EDUCATION

Texas also has a better sense of the role of the *Texas Standards for Teacher Education.* There is currently some contention between the Texas Education Agency and the university faculties over requirements for curricula and the faculty's traditional perception of their right to teach what they want. With all respect for that tradition, the agency believes that teacher education belongs in the context of a professional school, not a liberal arts program. In a professional program, there is a strong argument for accountability because we have to prepare teachers to teach students the mandated Essential Elements.

COMMUNICATION

Agency staff meet weekly with the Certification Division within the agency, trying to improve the consistency between the testing programs and the needs of hiring school districts. We also meet regularly with the colleges and universities to make certain that they understand what the testing program is attempting to accomplish and what the tests are like. We have found that teacher education faculty members are often unaware of aspects of the program that we in the agency take for granted. Last, as mentioned, the Essential Elements will be revised in 1988-89.

The Texas Education Agency, along with National Evaluation Systems, Inc., will be conducting topicality reviews at about that time to keep the test objectives and items consistent with revisions to the Essential Elements. The *Standards* are currently under review, so the administrative board of education can begin to work out any inconsistencies between the Essential Elements and those standards. In short, we are moving toward an integrated system of classroom instruction and teacher preparation, with test content reflecting both for prospective teachers.

State-Mandated Classroom Curricula and Certification Testing

Robert Gabrys

BASIS OF THE TESTING PROGRAM

In testing prospective teachers, West Virginia took its lead from the public school curriculum and viewed the whole issue of job relatedness very seriously. The state board began a total reform in education by establishing an educational program for students. That program defined what the student is expected to learn as a result of the entire K-12 educational process. The educational program is further defined by programs of study, such as mathematics, science, and reading. Each program was further divided into subareas of study, such as algebra, biology, and spelling. These subareas contained a series of learning outcomes (e.g., what specifically the student is to learn in Algebra I). The outcomes are at a higher level than instructional objectives, and so do not dictate to a teacher how he or she is to teach. West Virginia county school districts are then responsible for defining objectives for those learning outcomes, making the content more specific and related to local curriculum needs.

Test items are now being developed for the state-level learning outcomes. The items constitute an item bank to be used for diagnostic purposes in support of instruction. Teachers will be able to request test items from the state that relate to specific objectives that they are teaching. The resulting tests will thereby be customized to a particular teacher's needs as opposed to being a part of a statewide assessment system. The banks of items serve primarily the instructional purposes of teachers as opposed to being an evaluation of the public school structure at the state level.

IMPACT ON HIGHER EDUCATION

Parallel to this effort was one in higher education, wherein there are approved teacher education programs. The programs are defined for given subject areas, such as mathematics, paralleling public school programs of study. The areas of study are those subsets of mathematics that are covered in the public schools and are, therefore, present in the higher education mathematics curriculum.

The learning outcomes for public education are reflected in the higher education curriculum insofar as we are attempting to provide instruction to prospective teachers that is related to the content they will be responsible for teaching in the classroom. Hence, the higher education programs will prepare prospective teachers more appropriately.

JOB RELATEDNESS

The correlation of teacher education and public school curricula is further enhanced by the job relatedness of our testing of prospective teachers. The test items for prospective teachers reflect the learning outcomes for public education that were adopted by the State Board of Education. The learning outcomes describe what a student will learn; the teacher test objectives define the level of mathematics a teacher should know in order to teach those learning outcomes. Hence, the tests for prospective teachers do more than present a test that makes sure the seventh-grade teacher knows seventh-grade mathematics. West Virginia's testing program does not simply verify the teacher's knowledge of fractions, but also a level of content understanding that the teacher must have in order to teach children about fractions. Our validation approach derives directly from the state-mandated public school curriculum.

JOB RELATEDNESS AND TEACHER PREPARATION

This relationship between higher education and public school curricula caused a significant shift for higher education institutions because the teacher training curriculum had to reflect what goes on in public schools. One of the problems with this approach centers on whether the teacher preparation institutions may be reducing the level of their curriculum to match the status quo in the public schools. It was obviously not the intention of the State Board of Education to limit instruction in higher education to only those elements required in public school curriculum. To discourage that possibility, West Virginia eliminated all minimum credit-hour requirements. We encourage institutions of higher education to document that they are not simply teaching content at a level to cover the public school learning outcomes, but are extending beyond them in accordance with what their faculty think is important for a teacher in a given content field to know. Thus the teacher training programs are not limited by the state curriculum.

The correlational approach does allow us to track virtually every approved program for the adequacy of instruction, as a minimum requirement, and for delivery of the specific learning outcomes adopted by the State Board of Education for public schools.

IMPACT ON TEXTBOOK ADOPTION

One additional step West Virginia is implementing is to work on aligning the textbook adoption process and the state-mandated learning outcomes. We have established a link between the public school curriculum and the higher education training programs and are implementing one between the adopted textbooks and the learning outcomes.